Therapeutic Community

Past. Present. And Moving Forward

Fernando B. Perfas

Therapeutic Community

Cover Design by Rodolfo Loquinario, 2014

Published by:
Hexagram Publishing, Red Hook, N.Y.
Printed in the United States of America

ISBN-10:1500267058
ISBN-13:978-1500267056

Library of Congress Control Number: 2014911574
CreateSpace Independent Publishing Platform, North Charleston, SC

Other books by Fernando B. Perfas

Deconstructing the Therapeutic Community
Therapeutic Community: A Social System Perspective
Therapeutic Community: A Practice Guide

For

FJ, Mirabai, & Christian

Contents

Chapter 8: A Revitalized Treatment Agenda for
the Therapeutic Community. 135

List of Tables and Figures

Acknowledgment

To the following individuals who helped with this project and those who influenced me in my career:

Mirabai Perfas, a competent editor whose work has been invaluable in seeing through this project,

FJ Perfas, who helped with some of the editing work,

Rodolfo "Loqui" Loquinario, who designed the book cover,

Bob Garon, who introduced me to the TC,

Prof. Somnuck Rodprasert and Dr. Thongchai Uneklab, my friends and supporters in the early days of the TC project in Thailand,

Msgr. William O'Brien, who welcomed me to Daytop Village and provided a place dedicated to "helping man help himself," and

Last but not least, Mary Beth, my wife, who has been my companion in this TC journey,

My deepest thanks and appreciation!

Preface

The concept of the therapeutic community (TC) has been around for more than half a century. From its humble beginnings as an unorthodox approach to the treatment of drug addiction, it eventually became an accepted treatment model not only in the United States but across the globe. Although the TC continues to thrive in its true form in some community-based and prison settings, many of the second generation TCs that were established in the 1960s have undergone drastic transformations. While many drug abuse treatment programs are still using some elements of the TC, particularly the use of its structure in residential treatment programs, they are rarely identified as a TC. Instead, the TC has become absorbed into a new treatment paradigm called "behavioral health."

This trend is driven by the increasing integration of treatment for addiction and mental health due to the high rates of co-occurrence of both conditions. This phenomenon caught the TC community off guard and has complex ramifications from funding, treatment, and administration perspectives. What used to be separate treatment domains are now merging. The issue is no longer "Which came first, the chicken or the egg?" Now it is more a question of "Which is important, the chicken or the egg?" Incidentally, this shift took place during the waning days of the TC, when its staffing pattern moved from one in which the "ex-addict staff" had a greater role in the TC to one in which the professional staff predominantly started to call the shots. The shift was all about economics.

TC treatment, though proven effective, was considered to be too long. So began the hunt for a shortcut to drug treatment with the goal of saving money. To survive, the TC had to provide a shorter version of its treatment regardless of fidelity to practice and what is considered realistic treatment for addiction. Funders also started to demand for "evidence-based practices" and more credentialed professional staff to work in the drug treatment programs. This has resulted in TCs that are managed by professional staff who are knowledgeable in science-based interventions, but many are not familiar with how the TC works. The transition from the TC to behavioral health has resulted in more problems for the TC. As the emphasis shifted to "evidence-based practices," drug abuse treatment programs not only stopped training staff on the TC but incentives among professional staff to learn and increase proficiency on the TC also vanished. Given the current unfavorable economic conditions and the shift in treatment priorities, public drug abuse treatment programs continue to be under-funded and are finding it difficult to survive. The timing couldn't be worse as heroin abuse increases at an alarming epidemic rate, and substance abuse in general remains a major public health concern.

At the end of the day, all this shifting around has little to do with "really" treating addiction. Drug abuse treatment and government policy keep missing the boat. This is quite obvious by the lack of agreement on how to define addiction. Is it really a disease? Is it a personality quirk? Is it a moral defect? Is it a chronically relapsing condition? Currently, addiction is described as a "brain disease" and funding is being directed towards science-based and more cognitive behavioral approaches to treatment.

Despite the passing treatment fads, one fact remains. The twelve-step program has hardly changed since its beginning and continues to be the most popular, cost effective form of treatment. There is something to be learned from the success of Alcoholics Anonymous (AA) or Narcotics Anonymous (NA) in regards to addiction and its treatment. The structure that the twelve steps provide, the fellowship the group offers, the sense of meaning imbued on the recovery process, and the social support from members of all walks of life combine to constitute the social context of the twelve-step program. It is not rocket science and yet science cannot put its finger on why this system really works.

The parallel between the twelve-step program and the Therapeutic Community is clear. They are branches of the same tree. Both have elements of community and adhere to one fundamental principle: "Man helping man." Attention needs to be focused on the social context of both models. In this context, genuine relationships, bonding, and healthy attachments between and among people who are working towards a common goal are the most important elements of recovery. Most people who have recovered from substance abuse through the TC, and likely through AA as well, often remember important turning points in treatment in relation to the people who played a role in them and not so much the interventions. This touches the very core of addiction and the recovery from it: The importance of positive relationships.

The inclusion of attachment theory as a new paradigm for guiding the TC practice is less a shift in perspective than an elaboration on the soul of its treatment philosophy of "man helping man" and self-help. Attachment theory provides the narrative for explaining why the TC does what it does. The intuitive assumption that the roots of addiction run deep in the whole person and find ground in a fractured sense of self, failed relationships, inadequate means to control one's life, and a warped view of others, can now be made more explicit and find support in science.

Introduction

This book provides a broad stroke of the TC history and its dispersion around the world. An important question to consider is "How has the Therapeutic Community changed during its worldwide dispersion?" This can be a difficult question to consider as there is no one standardized version of the TC for addictions, otherwise known as the Concept-Based or American Hierarchical TC. To wit, there is the Italian TC model which was adopted from Daytop Village in New York by the *Centro di Solidarieta* (CEIS) in Italy and later made its way to countries in Latin America. Some European and Australian TCs are spin-offs of Phoenix House and Odyssey House in New York. The TC used in the Philippines in the 1970s was influenced by both Daytop Village and Phoenix House. Later, the Filipino model was adopted in Thailand as well as Malaysia and eventually influenced the TCs that formed in Indonesia, Singapore, and China. In the U.S., every TC is a version or a replica of the original concept that was developed in Synanon. This does not include TCs that are products of deliberate modifications to suit particular treatment populations, e.g., mentally-ill drug users, criminal justice drug offenders, adolescents, women, etc.

Although a consistent pattern of similarities has emerged wherever the TC has thrived, there are differences in TCs around the world that occur as a result of each unique locale. The goal of this book is to examine some of the factors that have shaped the transformations of the TC in the U.S. and around the world. The term "hybridization" is used to describe the transformations of the TC as it was adopted in various places and treatment settings. The term and concept is borrowed from the paleoanthropologist Chris Stringer (2012). Within the context of hybridization, it is possible to look into how the TC concepts, principles, and philosophies have been transformed, enhanced or diminished in its various forms.

This book first delineates the major components and practice principles of the TC as a basis for examining program consistency and fidelity to the TC concept and philosophy. These principles are the minimum requirements necessary for a program to be considered a TC and are similar to De Leon and Melnick (1993) "Essential Elements of the Therapeutic Community" with the main difference being that the principles are organized and couched in a language that is more practice oriented.

Following the outline of practice principles is an examination of how they have stood up under the pressure of adaptations or hybridization. How have the TC principles been kept intact while the TC form was modified to suit cultural tastes? What elements of the TC practice principles withstood the pressure of adaptations to become integrated into the host environment? These are questions that TCs across the world should try to examine and answer.

The TC is often described as using "Community-As-Method" as its treatment model. This is the cornerstone of the TC concept which is easy to grasp conceptually but difficult to put into practice. This book attempts to explain how this treatment model works by describing the functions of the TC social structure as well as the four overlapping operational functions which are necessary in structuring a successful TC.

Grounding the TC on psychological theories is not only an important task to undertake but is also necessary for the TC to continue to flourish. This book outlines a new agenda for revamping TC methodologies to make them consistent with evidence-based practices. Intricately linked to this task is the importance of emphasizing the bi-modal nature of the therapeutic community in that it is not only a method of intervention but is also a social system that provides the context for the TC. Hopefully this perspective enhances the understanding of the TC and how outcome studies may be designed to test its effectiveness.

Finally, this book outlines the current challenges that TCs are facing. The list focuses on issues that affect TCs in the United States and is by no means exhaustive.

An Overview of the History and Diffusion of the Therapeutic Community

What is a Therapeutic Community?

The term *Therapeutic community,* or TC for short, refers to a drug treatment approach that uses the community and its group dynamics for therapeutic purposes. Unlike the traditional medical-mental health model that emphasizes the therapeutic role of the professional as primary in treatment, the TC is largely a self-help model that emphasizes the therapeutic role of peer interactions in helping shape behavior, address psychological problems, challenge and modify faulty cognition, and acquire effective social and coping skills. Various definitions focus on certain aspects of the TC, such as its strong social learning character, its cognitive-behavioral elements, or the TC as a treatment model and a social system (Perfas, 2004). Some writers (Glaser, 1978; O'Brien & Perfas, 2005) trace the origin of the term and practice of "community" from the early Christian communes or Eastern monastic communities whose practices have parallels in modern TCs. Modern TCs for addictions implement a unique set of therapeutic tools that have evolved to address the major behavioral, psychological, cognitive, and social goals of treatment. However, due to ignorance and bad practice, some of the TCs highly evocative tools, such as the *encounter group*, *verbal haircut*, and *confrontation* have achieved some level of notoriety and controversy.

As a treatment model the TC utilizes a community approach to changing behavior and imparting pro-social values to members (referred to as residents) who suffer from different degrees of substance abuse and other behavioral problems. Most TCs have some or most of the following characteristics:

- An informal environment with a distinct communal atmosphere, in contrast to the formal environment of most treatment institutions,
- A social hierarchy of members which defines their status and scope of responsibility for maintaining the treatment community,
- A safe environment with established norms, values, and rules which define boundaries and expectations for members (including staff),
- A trans-disciplinary staff composed of both recovering or para-professional and professional staff,
- A daily structure with program activities that promote the maintenance and development of the community as well as various formal and informal therapeutic activities,
- A self-help and mutual help driven treatment also known as "peer-driven" treatment, and
- An established practice for shaping behavior, feeling, and thinking referred to as the "TC tools."

Two Types of Therapeutic Communities

There are two types of therapeutic communities. One is the *democratic therapeutic community* and the other is known as the *concept-based therapeutic community,* sometimes referred to as the *hierarchical TC* or the *TC for addictions.*

The Democratic Therapeutic Community

The democratic therapeutic community was started in the mid-1940s by a group of British Army medical officers to treat soldiers who had developed neurosis, known as "shell-shock syndrome," during the Second World War. At the time, the development of the TC model was considered a revolution in social psychiatry and was largely a psychiatric, hospital-based treatment. Maxwell Jones, a psychiatrist and one the early practitioners of the TC model, wrote several books about a brand of the democratic TC that he developed and popularized. The treatment later became known as the Maxwell Jones Model (Vandevelde, 1999). This psychiatric model was used largely to treat patients with mental illness.

The Concept-Based Therapeutic Community

The American model of the TC was started by Charles E. Dederich along with a group of alcoholics and heroin addicts who banded together to give up their addiction. Together they started *Synanon*. The story of Synanon is documented in a classic book, *Synanon: The Tunnel Back*, by Yablonsky (1965). Janzen (2001) provided a balanced account of the rise and eventual fall of Synanon. He acknowledged Synanon's unique contributions as a social movement and a radical approach to the treatment of social maladies, particularly addiction.

In 1958, financially broke and twice divorced due to alcoholism, Charles E. Dederich begun holding weekly meetings modeled after the Alcoholics Anonymous (AA) in his own place. In these weekly meetings, he employed a style of group therapy that was highly confrontational. The intense group process demanded members to be absolutely honest regarding their substance abuse and addictive behavioral patterns. The group process also facilitated a high level of member cohesiveness and was successful in helping members to abstain from substance abuse. By practicing honesty in these groups away from distractions of outside influences, members were able to abstain from substance abuse for an extended period of time which they had previously been unable to achieve. Noting the success of the group and the importance of removing members from the context of their substance abusing lifestyle, Dederich began to rent a place in Santa Monica, California where members could live together; thus, the therapeutic community for addictions was born. The small community grew and eventually became known as

Synanon, and the TC model that developed there was known as the *concept-based TC* or the *hierarchical TC.* The stellar rise of Synanon and its communal approach to the treatment of addiction, which was considered at the time a breakthrough in the treatment of heroin addiction, ended in a precipitous fall when Dederich turned the organization into a cult-like movement. The serious problems in the Synanon's leadership became apparent around the second half of the 1970s. The treatment elements and techniques which were developed in Synanon during its golden years in the early 1960s were later adopted by the next generations of therapeutic communities.

The psychiatric-based democratic TC of the UK predated the concept-based TC by almost two decades and they developed independently. However, both share a fundamental philosophy of "community as healer." Throughout the years, both models have undergone significant transformations as each model has been adopted and adapted to treat different types of client populations. For example, there are democratic TCs developed to treat prisoners with substance abuse backgrounds, and there are also adaptations of concept-based TCs to treat mentally-ill clients with substance abuse histories. In Europe, in particular, there are TCs that have been strongly influenced by both models. These TCs combine what the developers viewed as the best elements of each model.

The Therapeutic Tools of the Concept-Based TC

The TC model that this book focuses on is the concept-based TC or the TC for addictions. Many of the therapeutic tools that have become popular in most concept-based TCs were first introduced at Synanon. Yablonsky (1965) provided the following rough account of these tools in his book:

1 The *Game* or *synanon* – the prototype of the Encounter Group used in subsequent TCs

2 *Seminar* - a daily gathering in the community used as a forum for intellectual discussions and exchange of ideas on a chosen subject

3 *Verbal Haircut* - a form of reprimand delivered by peers and staff to an offending resident

4 *Learning Experience* - a task performed as restitution designed to teach a "lesson" to an offending resident for serious misbehavior

5 *The Fire Place Scene* - employed to address violations of the TC's Cardinal Rules, particularly substance use; this later became known as the General Meeting

6 *Indoctrination* or *Initial Interview* - a ritual for admitting a prospective resident which is conducted by a panel of peers and staff to explore treatment motivation

7 *The Hierarchical Structure* - the social organization of a TC

8 *The Concepts or Philosophies* - embody the philosophies and values of the TC, i.e., "no free lunch," "act-as-if," "pride in quality," etc.

9 *Walking Around Money (WAM)* – a small amount of money that residents are allowed to carry in the community; this is a privilege that must be earned

10 *Cop-out* - when a resident voluntarily confesses to breaking a community rule, such as "taking a drink," "bringing in contraband," etc.; this later became known as the Guilt Session

11 *Morning Meeting* - a daily ritual of community gathering to review community issues, build community spirit, and chart out the course of the day

12 *The Trip* - an extended form of group therapy and the precursor to the *Marathon Group* which is a continuous group process that lasts for at least 36 to 76 hours

13 *Role-Model* - the concept of senior community residents teaching younger residents by example

14 *Confrontation* - an incisive inquiry into a resident's behavior, attitude, and thinking; used to raise awareness regarding the resident's unconscious motivation and demands personal accountability for a behavior or attitude

15 *The Concept of Family* - used to describe the social affiliation within the community and the social organization of the TC

16 *Structure* – used to describe the daily schedule as well as the social hierarchy of the community

17 *Job Functions* - sets of tasks organized by work departments
18 *Stages of Growth* - the precursor to the Treatment Phases that residents go through starting from Orientation and culminating in Reentry and Aftercare
19 *Saturday Night Meeting* or *Open House* - a weekly social gathering where TC supporters who are not residents are invited to mingle with the TC members
20 *Big Brother* or *Big Sister* - a new resident's mentor who helps him/her adjust to the TC
21 *Status Probe* – a term used for when a resident seeks and accounts for a job position in the community

The Birth of the Second Generation Therapeutic Communities

In the 1960s through the 70s, several members left the community when Dederich turned Synanon into a cult-like organization. Many started "second generation" TCs modeled after Synanon which helped to spawn the growth of the TC in the U.S. and Canada. TCs like Delancey Street in San Francisco, X-Calay Community and Portage in Canada, Habilitat in Hawaii and many others all have roots in Synanon. However, it was in the Northeastern part of the U.S. that several of these second generation TCs proliferated. Daytop Village was the first Synanon "spin-off" in New York and was followed by others such as Phoenix House, Odyssey House, Samaritan Village and several smaller houses. Marathon House was formed in Rhode Island. Gaudenzia House was founded in Philadelphia by a group of ex-addict staff who broke away from Daytop, and Daytop Inc. began in Connecticut. TCs in other parts of the U.S. included Gateway House in Chicago, Concept House in Florida, SHAR in Detroit, Walden House in San Francisco, Amity Foundation in Arizona, and many others.

The second generation TCs kept most of the original Synanon treatment methods. Although some of these TCs were organized with help from professionals or civic-minded community leaders, the clinical operations were often left in the hands of recovered, ex-addict staff members who made up the majority of the TC staff at the time. The professional staff were generally relegated to an auxiliary or supportive role.

There were two fundamental differences that separated these TCs from Synanon: the nature of membership and the legal structure of the TC organization. While Synanon eventually became a "closed" TC, where lifetime membership was required, the second generation TCs adopted an "open" approach to treatment where the goal was the eventual reintegration of the recovering addict back into society. Dederich saw himself as the absolute "ruler" of his realm which had catastrophic consequences for the lack of checks and balances. Under his leadership, Synanon eventually became corrupted and departed from its original treatment goal. The second generation TCs have avoided this pitfall by implementing a Board of Trustees. The Board has the authority to override or dismiss the TC leader, a prerogative that had been used, though sparingly, to re-shape some TCs.

Today, these TCs have changed and many do not identify themselves as a TC anymore but instead identify with the treatment model called "behavioral health." However, they continue to employ some elements of the TC, especially the use of the TC structure in their residential programs. Many of these programs have been transformed by the increasing emphasis on a medical model or have adopted a "softer" version of the TC in response to the rise in the number of substance abuse clients with co-occurring mental health disorders. The traditional TC's highly confrontational approach to treatment was considered unsuitable for these clients.

The Major Concepts of the Therapeutic Community

The following are some of the major concepts and belief system of the TC:

Addiction involves the person as a whole and manifests itself in different levels of dysfunction.

The TC's view of addiction does not focus on the drugs or substances per se. Instead, it looks to the individual to find the root of the problem. An individual's substance abuse is a symptom of an underlying disorder that manifests itself in different levels of dysfunction. The level of dysfunction will influence the level of treatment that each resident of the TC receives. Individuals who, despite their dysfunction associated with their substance abuse and addictive lifestyle, were able to maintain some level of psychosocial functioning will benefit from the rehabilitative influences of the TC; whereas, individuals whose substance abuse is accompanied by serious deficits in healthy upbringing, a lack of education and job skills, the presence of co-occurring mental health problems, limited or absence of social support system, and criminogenic propensities will require a higher level of services in addition to the socializing influences of the TC.

Treatment from addiction involves a recovery process.

The goal of treatment is not only abstinence from mind-altering substances but also to live a safe and responsible life, or "right living." The TC utilizes a recovery-oriented treatment process where the goal of treatment is to help each resident achieve sobriety and lead a safe and drug-free lifestyle. TC residents learn the necessary skills to prevent drug relapse and live a life free from crime, unhealthy associations, and unsafe practices. Residents are expected to achieve a certain level of emotional maturity from their treatment experiences. A resident may or may not achieve the ultimate goal of recovery upon completion of treatment in TC; however, it is expected that what he has achieved or learned from treatment will ultimately lead him down the path of sobriety.

Treatment in the TC can be viewed as a jump-start to the recovery process, whereby the resident learns the basics of sobriety, develops self-awareness, and acquires coping and survival skills.

Recovery involves acquiring and internalizing pro-social values that support the recovery process.

Many TC values and philosophies are reflected in various mantras that are echoed throughout the community. Philosophies such as "No free lunch;" "You alone can do it, but you can't do it alone;" "You can't keep it unless you give it away;" "What goes around, comes around;" "honesty;" "pride in quality;" "responsible concern;" etc., help to shape a new way of thinking for residents living in a TC. These concepts serve as reminders that to give up addiction one must give up street and prison values and embrace a different lifestyle and value system. The TC believes that to give up drugs or addiction the addict must cultivate or reacquire a moral sense. The entire philosophy of 12-step program is based on achieving a higher level of morality, one that is often equated with spirituality. Dederich, during the early days of Synanon, observed that absolute honesty concerning the use of substances was necessary to protect the resident from relapsing to an addictive lifestyle. The highly confrontational group sessions that he implemented during the formative years of Synanon were focused on an unrelenting search for the truth and honesty. The phenomenological significance of that quest as the ultimate goal of the group process had surprising results. Hardcore addicts and alcoholics were able to take control of their addiction. The TC concepts and values are considered important parts of the TC Practice Principles (See Chapter 3).

Healing from addiction occurs in the context of "community" or helping oneself while helping others.

The concept of "community as method" defines the treatment philosophy of the TC in which the group or community dynamic is the primary source of therapy or healing. TC residents are expected to always lend a helping hand to each other as part of the treatment process. They are taught to look to the community to meet their needs, get support, and develop an understanding of their own problems through their interactions with peers. By working with members of the community, including staff, residents are assisted in finding solutions to their problems and difficulties. The social learning potential inherent in the interactions among community members within the structured environment of the TC is harnessed to influence behavioral, attitudinal, psychological, and cognitive shifts from the residents' addictive propensities. Feedback is shared during group and community meetings, individual sessions, and seminars which help residents develop insight about their behavior, thinking, and feeling. This concept is also included as one of the essential Practice Principles of the TC (See Chapter 3).

Self-help and mutual help is encouraged among community members who play a dual role of "client-therapist."

A social learning context is fostered within the TC when a resident effectively plays the role of therapist by providing social support to a peer who is in distress or by holding a peer accountable for inappropriate behavior. The roles may reverse when the same resident has his turn as the recipient of good counsel or when he becomes the subject of a "confrontation" by his peers. Since social interactions among residents constantly shift between counselor and counselee, depending on the situation, residents are provided with different perspectives by which to view their problems.

It is through this process that residents are able to become deeply familiar with each other and provide emotional support for one another. The same process applies when they take turns "confronting or challenging" each other to address observed negative or unproductive behaviors. There is tacit agreement among residents that everyone is flawed and it is the responsibility of each resident to point out the unhealthy behaviors that he observes among his peers. This practice is not about passing judgment on one another but is focused on raising awareness of behaviors or attitudes that need to be addressed.

Staff members are viewed as role models and rational authority.

The staff's professional status and social standing in the TC has significant influence on the residents. They are viewed as role models who are expected to practice what they preach. The way in which staff members conduct themselves within as well as outside of the TC determines their credibility in the community more than their academic credentials.

Closely related to the concept of "role model" is the concept of "rational authority" which refers to how staff members relate with and exercise authority over residents. Initially, residents often have unfavorable views and attitudes towards authority figures. This negative stance towards authority stems from the fact that many have had significant negative experiences with authority figures, such as parental figures, school officials, law enforcement officers, prison officers, judges, etc. To overcome their belief that they have been treated unfairly or victimized by people who should have protected them residents must have a different experience with authority figures in the TC. Staff and community members with authority must be perceived as fair, firm, consistent, and caring. This TC concept is also included as one of the Practice Principles of the TC (See Chapter 3).

TC staff members assume a dual role which involves clinical and operational functions within a trans-disciplinary model.
Staffing in TCs nowadays often includes a mix of professional and para-professionals with different academic and training backgrounds. They carry out various functions to support the TC in both clinical and operational capacities within a trans-disciplinary staffing model. Clinical functions include the provision and facilitation of treatment interventions and services (e.g., screening and assessment, treatment planning, counseling, group facilitation, etc.) while operational functions involve implementation and supervision of the TC processes (e.g., resident social structure, surveillance, peer interventions, morning meetings, daily schedule, house meetings, conflict management or encounter groups, seminars, etc.).

In recent years the distribution of these roles varies between TCs. In some TCs the staffing model requires these two major functions to be carried out by different sets of staff, while in others each staff member carries out both functions.

The Diffusion of the Concept-Based or TC for Addictions

From the mid-1960s through the 1970s there was growing interest in concept-based TCs from European, Asian, Scandinavian, South American, Middle Eastern professionals and paraprofessionals. Daytop Village, Phoenix House, and Odyssey House, all in New York, became popular destinations to learn about the TC. Before long, there were Daytop Germany, Daytop Sweden, Phoenix Houses in England and Norway, and an Odyssey House in Australia. These overseas TCs were all organized by professionals who visited TCs in the U.S. or ex-addict staff sent overseas from the U.S. These TCs were generally not corporate branches, only copies of the U.S. models.

Europe

In the early 1960s, professionals from the U.K. began visiting TC's in New York, particularly Daytop Village, to learn about the American TC. Some stayed for a few months to immerse themselves in the community. In 1968, Alpha House opened in Portsmouth as the first concept-based TC in England. This was followed by the opening of Phoenix House London the following year. Not long after, the Ley Community and Suffolk House started operation. These TCs were highly influenced by the American concept-based TC (Warren-Holland, 1977). They subscribed to the TC's basic tenet of viewing addiction as a disorder of the whole person, and that substance abuse is the symptom of an underlying problem manifested in the person's behavior, attitude, feeling, and thinking. These TCs were highly structured and members were organized into a hierarchical social structure in which there were various job positions. Members could aspire to fill these positions through the adoption and practice of pro-social behavior, acculturation to the TC lifestyle, and the pursuit of a "change plan."

One of the influential TCs outside of England was Emiliehoeve in The Hague, Netherlands. It was founded in 1972, and during its first few months of operations followed a democratic TC model for clients with psychiatric disorders. The organizers were initially concerned that the American model was too rigid and authoritarian for the liberal society of the Netherlands. It did not take long for them to realize that the democratic TC practices were unsuitable for the type of clients they were treating. When the staff of Emiliehoeve saw the success of Phoenix House in London, they eventually adopted the American concept-based model. Emiliehoeve was instrumental in influencing the establishment of several TCs not only in the Netherlands but also in several European countries, such as Belgium, Switzerland, Italy, Germany, Sweden, Austria, Greece, and others. Besides Emiliehoeve, there were other independent TCs in the Netherlands that started from the Maxwell Jones democratic model and later evolved into a concept-based TC. The same is true with Vallmotorp in Sweden, a school that eventually established its own concept-based TC, which was patterned after Daytop Village, called Daytop Sweden (Kooyman, 2001). In the early 1980s, Vallmotorp was instrumental in helping to establish the Thai Ministry of Public Health's Thanyarak Hospital TC in Rangsit, Thailand.

In Italy, Rome's *Centro Italiano di Solidarieta* (C.E.I.S), a concept-based TC, had far-reaching influences in the dispersion of the TC in Italy, Spain, parts of Europe, and several South American countries. Its organizers learned about Daytop Village during a visit to Emiliehoeve in 1976. After organizing and hosting the Third World Conference of Therapeutic Communities (WFTC) in Rome in 1978, CEIS opened their first TC in 1979 as a program called *Progetto Uomo* (Project Humanity). This organization had strong ties with the Catholic Church and was responsible for the spread of the TC throughout most of Italy. Around the same time, the CEIS Training Institute was established to train Italian TC staff as well as others from foreign countries. Two directors from Daytop Village in New York were sent to assist in the development of the TC and provide training. Another staff member from a TC in Eagleville Hospital of Pennsylvania joined them and worked as an instructor at the Training Institute. The CEIS TC was notable for integrating a strong family therapy component into its TC model. Although CEIS dominated the TC landscape in Italy, there were also TCs that were established independently. One of these TCs was *Cascina Verde* of Milan. It was established in 1974 and predated the CEIS TC program (Kooyman, 2001).

Many concept-based TCs in Europe developed from what were originally psychiatric-based treatment programs as was the case with Norway's Vexthuset which was established in 1982. Phoenix House Norway was established with help from Phoenix House London. The same is true of Phoenix House Germany which later became Daytop Germany. Daytop Village and Phoenix House were the two New York-based TCs that had influenced the growth of concept-based TCs in

Europe. Like most third generation TCs, the European TCs that developed in the 1970s were largely initiated and staffed by medical-mental health professionals. In many cases, these TC's have features of a psychiatric model infused with the culture and practices of the concept-based TC.

Many professional staff from foreign countries traveled to the U.S. or to other well-established concept-based TCs in Europe and took "the Concept" back with them. These TCs had yet to include ex-addict staff that was so prevalent in the U.S.-based TCs at the time as government authorities were reluctant to accept ex-addicts as dependable staff (Kooyman, 2001). This was not uncommon among TCs that were pioneered outside of the U.S. during that period of time.

In Eastern Europe, Poland has the longest tradition of therapeutic communities aimed at rehabilitation and prolonged drug abstinence. In 1977, a treatment facility for drug addicts that incorporated a TC was set up within a psychiatric hospital. Starting in 1978, Monar Centers, which were self-help agricultural TCs, spread throughout Poland. Their structure was remarkably similar to that of Synanon in the United States although there is no known prior contact between the two programs. In Yugoslavia and Czechoslovakia, professionals established TCs for alcoholics with a similar mutual help ideology (Kooyman, 1992).

Australasia

The American concept-based TC reached Australia through the establishment of Odyssey House in Campbelltown, New South Wales by Walter McGrath. McGrath, whose son had died from a heroin overdose, travelled to North America looking for a treatment model suitable for Australians. His search brought him to Odyssey House in New York. When he returned to Australia he established the Australian Odyssey House in 1977 (Lloyd and O'Callaghan, 2001). Prior to Odyssey House, the first residential rehabilitation program in Australia that came close to the self-help TC model was WHOS (We Help Ourselves) which was established in New South Wales in 1972.

Mirakai was an Australian drug treatment program that catered to troubled youth. It was established in 1971 with a treatment model that became increasingly aligned with the therapeutic community over the course of time. The Buttery, a rehabilitation program that was established in 1972, was originally a predominantly Christian-based program that also served trouble youth but through the years it evolved to become more of a concept-based TC. It eventually became one of the most influential TCs in Australia and was instrumental in the formation of other TCs. As TCs spread across Australia, it was only a matter of time before the treatment model made its way to neighboring New Zealand. The following account of the history of TCs in New Zealand was taken from the Matua Raki report for the Ministry of Health (2012):

Odyssey House in Auckland, New Zealand opened its first TC in 1981 as one of the first concept-based TC in the country. Currently, it offers a wide range of programs and services in eight treatment centers located in Auckland City, Manukau City, and Whangarei. The treatment centers provide services for adults of all ages and drug abuse clients with co-occurring issues. They also provide residential family programs that include children younger than 12 years old as well as transitional houses. Odyssey House Trust Christchurch offers a coed youth residential and day program as well as a long-term adult program. A transitional house for men is also available.

Established in 1984, Higher Ground Drug Rehabilitation Trust provides treatment for clients with severe substance abuse history. Its 18-week residential program combines the TC with 12-Step recovery principles. Higher Ground also provides aftercare services that include individual and group counseling.

Care NZ is a prison-based drug rehabilitation program that uses the TC in its drug treatment units. Established in 1997, there is a TC in one women's prison and seven TC programs in the men's prisons of the North and South Islands. The TCs in these programs have been modified to meet the Department of Corrections' requirements. It is one of few Correctional-based TCs that has a re-entry stage and includes a family program to support aftercare.

The Moana House in Dunedin is a TC that serves a special population of repeat offenders. Established in 1984, it has a bi-cultural program consisting of four stages. As residents progress through the treatment stages they are faced with increasing levels of expectations but there is no set timeframe for each stage.

In 1986, the Australasian Therapeutic Community Association (ATCA) was formed. It represented all shades of TCs providing them with a voice and a source of advocacy. Today, ATCA is an umbrella organization that represents TCs across Australia and New Zealand. The evolution of TCs in Australasia was influenced by both the U.S. Concept-based TC and the U.K. Democratic TC models (ATCA publication, 2013).

Asia and the Middle East

From the 1960s until the early 70s, heroin was the major drug of abuse in the Philippines. There was a serious heroin epidemic raging in Manila but there was no known effective treatment for those addicted to heroin. Addicted individuals from wealthy families were treated in psychiatric units of private hospitals, while those from poor families often ended up in prisons for drug-related crimes or were confined in one of the law enforcement agencies' operated drug rehabilitation centers.

In 1971, Bob Garon, a Catholic mission priest, started the first Filipino private drug abuse prevention and treatment program called Drug Abuse Research Foundation, Inc. (DARE) in Manila. He established the first concept-based TC in the Philippines with help from an ex-heroin addicted person. DARE's first TC house was named *Bahay Pag-asa* (House of Hope). DARE became the largest and most successful non-government drug treatment program in the Philippines. It would eventually play a major role helping to spread the TC throughout Southeast Asia.

Garon sent Mario, a Filipino heroin ex-addict, to the U.S. to observe and learn the TC. He left Manila in 1971 for New York. After spending a month visiting Daytop Village and Phoenix House in New York, Mario returned to Manila bringing the TC concept back with him. He was to become the first TC graduate to be trained as staff at DARE. Over the next few months he worked to implement the TC concept into *Bahay Pag-asa* program and educate the residents about the concept. By early 1972, DARE had a thriving TC of over thirty residents with a core of enthusiastic senior residents as well as a well-trained professional staff as support personnel.

After the declaration of Martial Law in September, 1972 by then Filipino dictator Marcos and the subsequent execution of Lim Seng, the notorious Chinese drug trafficker, the heroin market dried up in the Philippines. To avoid arrest by the Military Police, many heroin addicts sought admission to Garon's DARE program. Seemingly overnight, DARE Philippines grew to include several treatment facilities which were scattered in and around the Metro Manila area.

In its heyday, DARE had over five hundred residents in any given day. To support its operations, Garon established the DARE Industries, a consulting business that specialized in advertising and motivational training. Bob Garon, and a team of DARE residents as account executives, did not have any difficulty recruiting large business corporations for customers. With the help of DARE Industries, DARE Philippines was largely self-sufficient and did not have to depend on government subsidies or grants. It remained free from government interference for several years, allowing it the freedom to adopt and experiment with the TC model. DARE TC had several staff who were graduates of the DARE program and eventually established their own TCs or helped to develop other TC programs. Thriving TCs in the Philippines such as the Seagull's Flight, the SELF Foundation, and the faith-based Nazarene TC have all been influenced by the DARE TC.

****

In the mid-1970s, a German Catholic missionary based in Malaysia came to Manila to learn about DARE and experience the TC firsthand. When he returned to Malaysia he introduced the TC to a drug program known as *Pusat Pertolongan* in Ipoh, Malaysia. *Pusat Pertolongan* became the first Malaysian TC, and in its early years it received help from Filipino ex-addict staff members who were sent by DARE Philippines. Some Malaysian residents and professional staff were also sent to Manila for treatment and/or training. *Pusat Pertolongan* treated many residents who eventually went on to be trained as staff members. Some of these TC graduates later established their own TCs. One of which is the *Pengasih* TC in Kuala Lumpur. *Pengasih* is the most successful and influential Malaysian TC and was established by a graduate of *Pusat* who also received training from Daytop Village in New York. *Pengasih* has also provided treatment to clients from Indonesia in its treatment facilities in Kuala Lumpur. Indonesian parents of clients who were treated in *Pengasih* had organized themselves into a Parents' Association and eventually established their own TC in Indonesia.

The *Pingasih* TC has been a model for several Islamic TC programs in Asia. From Malaysia the TC traveled to neighboring Singapore. Singapore's *Pertapis* TC was developed by a Malaysian graduate of *Pusat Pertolongan* who also received training from Daytop. He later moved to Indonesia to work in a few Indonesian TCs. Indonesian TCs, such as the *Kasih Mulia*, descended from the Malaysian TC as well as TCs in Islamic countries of Brunei and Afghanistan.

In 1979, the DARE program in Manila loaned two of its program directors to a U.S.-based Catholic community with missions in Thailand for the purpose of starting a TC. Two years prior, a group of four Thai heroin addicts came for treatment and training in DARE. They were accompanied by two Thai sisters from the mission who also came to train with DARE. They all returned home to Bangkok with the two Filipino directors in 1979 to help form the first TC in Thailand. Established in the Province of Samut Songkram, sixty kilometers from Bangkok, the *Sungkirt Mai* or Rebirth TC opened its doors to Thai addicts in October, 1979. The first licensed TC in Thailand, to this day Rebirth remains the largest private TC in Thailand that provides treatment for both men and women. Some of its graduates have gone on to become paraprofessionals in the addiction field or start their own TC program.

In 1982, Thanyarak Hospital sent a team of medical and mental health staff to Daytop Sweden for training. Thanyarak Hospital was run by the Department of Medical Services under the Thai Ministry of Public Health and was the oldest treatment center for heroin addiction in Thailand. Led by the director of Thanyarak Hospital, the team spent a few months in Sweden to learn the TC methods. The director was a psychiatrist who had assisted the Filipino staff of Rebirth in obtaining their treatment license from the Thai Ministry of Public Health. Today, Thanyarak Hospital operates a large detoxification unit, six TC houses, an outpatient clinic, and a short-term TC. There are also currently TCs run by the Department of Medical Services operating in several provinces.

In the early 90s, the Departments of Corrections of Thailand and Malaysia each launched an initiative to develop TCs in prisons. Daytop International, with funding from the U.S. International Narcotics and Law Enforcement Affairs (INL), assisted in training personnel and extending technical assistance in organizing the TC inside the prisons. Daytop trainers went to Bangkok and Kuala Lumpur to conduct a series of training, and several corrections officers came to Daytop in New York for further training. A few years later, the Parole and Probation Administration of the Philippines embarked on the first criminal justice training on the TC that included law enforcement treatment centers, the Bureau of Corrections, and the Bureau of Jail Management and Penology.

In the 1990s, there was a great deal of interest in learning about the TC by other Asian and Middle Eastern countries that were plagued with the rising problem of drug abuse. These countries included India, Pakistan, China, Sri Lanka, Bangladesh, Nepal, Vietnam, Laos, South Korea, Japan, Egypt, Iran, Lebanon, and many others. Mental health professionals, religious leaders, ex-addict paraprofessionals, and government officials, who were involved in the control and treatment of drug abuse in these regions, paid visits to Daytop Village in New York to learn about the TC. Some spent a few months as interns in the Daytop program and then returned home to establish their own TC. By the late 1990s, TCs have been established in India, Pakistan, Nepal, China, Sri Lanka, Bangladesh, the Maldives, including Egypt, Lebanon, Israel, and Iran. All of them were patterned after the Daytop TC model.

Also in the 1990s, religious sisters from the Coptic Church in Egypt, who had visited Daytop Village in New York, established their own version of the TC. Iran has a successful government-funded TC program which was initiated by professionals who visited Daytop. In 1989, *Oum el Nour* had its humble beginning as a drug treatment program serving drug addicts in Lebanon. By the 1990s, it had grown into a viable therapeutic community patterned after the Daytop program. In 2007, *Cenacle de La Lumiere* was established just outside of Beirut. It is a faith-based drug program that serves both adult and adolescent clients. Influenced by the older Lebanese TC, *Oum el Nour, Cenacle* had successfully developed its own TC.

By the new millennium, the TC had come to the attention of Catholic sisters who were operating an orphanage in Seoul, South Korea. In the early 2000s, they organized a group of religious, professionals, and academics who were involved in the treatment of alcohol and substance abuse to visit Daytop Village in the U.S. They spent some time studying the Daytop residential programs in upstate New York and New Jersey. In response to the various Korean professionals who were regularly visiting Daytop, a team of staff from Daytop International traveled to South Korea to conduct workshops on the TC methods. The Korean Federation of Therapeutic Communities (KFTC) was later formed. In the last four years, groups of Korean undergraduate students from INHA and Handong Universities have come to the U.S. for six weeks of their summer to participate in trainings and internships at Daytop. Organized by Professor Mihyoung Lee of INHA University, this has been a successful program for training and preparing nursing and social science students for a career in public health and social services.

Around the same time that the South Koreans took interest in the Daytop TC, a small group of Japanese academics and recovering addicts also turned their attention to learning about the TC. Since then TCs have been established in Japan, and the Japanese have been regular participants in TC conferences held in the region.

To facilitate the exchange of ideas and cross-training of staff, the Asian Federation of Therapeutic Communities (AFTC) was established in Bangkok in the mid 1990s. It has since hosted several regional conferences on the TC. These events have become the major gatherings where

TC practitioners in the region are able to exchange views and ideas in the development and practice of the TC.

South America

From the late 1980s through the 1990s, the TC started to spread to Latin American countries, such as Argentina, Uruguay, Colombia, Peru, Ecuador, and Brazil. With help from the Italian CEIS, which brought its training program to Latin America, the TC was able to take root in the region. The program also had the support of professionals who had visited Daytop Village in the U.S. as well as those who had attended conferences organized by the World Federation of Therapeutic Communities (WFTC) and the Latin American Federation of Therapeutic Communities. TCs in Argentina, such as *El Reparo, Viaje de Vuelta, Programa Andres, Programa Cambio* and *Volver a Vivir*, were all established in the early 1990s. Like the TCs in the U.S., many were saddled with the additional problem of treating drug abusers who also suffered from the HIV/AIDS virus which ran rampant during the period.

A series of TC trainings, which included several private and government agencies, was held in Lima, Peru in the mid-1990s. *Instituto Libre Mundo*, a program for homeless children in Peru, established its TC for adolescents in 1993. Many of the privately operated TCs in Peru were inspired by the work of CEIS in Italy and the efforts of the Catholic priest, Fr. Gabriel Mejia, who headed the *Federacion Latinoamericana de Comunidades Terapeuticas* (Latin American Federation of Therapeutic Communities). He is also currently the head of the pioneering TC in Colombia under *Fundacion Hogares Claret*. As the primary leader of the Latin American Federation of Therapeutic Communities, Fr. Mejia has actively promoted the TC in many Latin American countries.

Also in the early 90s, Fr. Harold Rahm, S.J., established a TC in Campañas, Brazil called the *Promotional Association for Prayer and Work (APOT)*. Fr. Rahm's APOT program received special training on TC from Daytop International, including some of his staff whom he sent to train in Daytop Village in the U.S. When the reorganized juvenile rehabilitation program for offenders was launched in the mid-2000s under the newly established *Fundacion Casa*, Daytop International was invited to conduct a series of training to train treatment and corrections officers in implementing the TC. Around the same time period, Fr. Mejia's Fundacion Hogares Claret, along with other private TCs, received a series of TC trainings in Medellin, Colombia to upgrade their TC practice.

Daytop's influence in Latin American TCs was cemented by a training program that was funded by the U.S. Department of State, International Narcotics and Law Enforcement Affairs (INL). A team of Daytop International staff members started training TC professionals from Argentina and Uruguay in the early 1990s. Similar TC trainings were later held in Lima, Peru in the mid-1990s. These trainings included several private and government treatment agencies in Peru. Around the same time, a comprehensive TC training was held in Quito, Ecuador for private and government programs, including prison-based TCs. This was followed by a similar training about the TC in the early 2000s. The National Directorate for Psychosocial Rehabilitation in Ecuador received several trainings to help organize TCs within the prison system across the country.

A series of TC training was also held in Central American countries such as Guatemala and El Salvador, which included several member countries of the Organization of American States (OAS) beginning in the early 1990s. The latest of these trainings were held in Guatemala a couple of years ago.

Africa

In 1997, a TC called *Horizon's Halfway House* was established as the first TC in the Western Cape, South Africa. A year later, the *Orient TC* was founded under the auspices of the Muslim Judicial Council. A few years later in 2004, *Lighthouse on the Horizon* was established in Johannesburg by an ex-addict as its director, and who later became a health care professional. In 2006, the Neuropsychiatric Hospital in Abeokuta, Nigeria, invited a team of professionals from Daytop International to conduct training on the TC model to a group of hospital staff as well as representatives from other Nigerian health and social agencies. In the last four years, following a series of INL-funded Daytop International TC trainings in

Kenya, there has been an increased interest from Kenya and neighboring countries to develop their own TC programs.

Clearly, the TC movement has attracted leaders with diverse backgrounds. For example, *CEIS* in Italy was led by a clergy and a layman. *APOT* in Brazil, *Fundacion Hogares Claret* in Colombia, *Freedom House* in Nepal, *APON* in Bangladesh, *Kasih Mulia* in Indonesia and many others were founded by Catholic priests. *Pengasih* in Malaysia, *Seagull Flight* and *SELF Foundation* in the Philippines, *Pertapis* in Indonesia, *Shafa House* in India, *Lighthouse on the Horizon* in South Africa, just to mention a few, were started by ex-addicts. *Mithuru Mithuro Movement* in Sri Lanka was established by a Buddhist monk. *Emiliehoeve* in the Netherlands, *Thanyarak Hospital TC* in Thailand, *Logros TC* in a prison in Guayaquil, Ecuador, and *Daytop Kunming* in China were only some examples of many TCs that were established and led by a medical professional. *Orient TC* in South Africa was established with help from a school teacher, and *Odyssey House* in Australia was started by a former businessman.

The American Global Drug Demand Reduction Program, the Colombo Plan, and the World Federation of Therapeutic Communities

Word of mouth and professional connections were important factors that contributed to the global diffusion of the TC in the last four decades. The two most important sources of TC information that contributed to the spread of the TC were the regular conferences organized by the World Federation of Therapeutic Communities (WFTC) and the global drug demand reduction program under the U.S. State Department's INL.

Through their international drug demand reduction program, INL funded the spread of the TC in Asia, Latin America, and other parts of the world. Daytop International, a division of Daytop Village, received grants from INL for many years allowing this agency to teach about the TC, host ex-addicts and professional staff in their internship program, assist developing countries in forming a drug treatment infrastructure, and provide study tours to the Daytop program in New York for drug policy-makers, treatment professionals, and program executives from developing countries.

In the 90s, TC trainings were conducted using INL grants in several Asian countries such as Thailand, the Philippines, China, Malaysia, Singapore, Indonesia, Vietnam, Laos, and Pakistan, including some countries in Central Asia. These trainings helped spread the TC in the region. Training programs were also provided in Latin American countries such as Argentina, Uruguay, Peru, Brazil, Ecuador, and Colombia. Similar training programs on the TC were held in Eastern European countries, such as Poland, Hungary, and Russia.

The Drug Advisory Program (DAP) of Colombo Plan Bureau, a regional development agency based in Colombo, Sri Lanka, also used INL funding for regional training programs provided by Daytop International for community-based TC as well as criminal justice and prison-based TCs. Colombo Plan's DAP continues to receive funding from INL and has extended its training capabilities to include drug prevention training in addition to its training for treatment professionals in Asia. Through Daytop International and the Colombo Plan, INL has helped to fund drug abuse-related conferences for more than two decades, including conferences organized by the Asian Federation of Therapeutic Communities (AFTC). INL has also provided funding for several TC conferences in Latin America under the auspices of the Federation of Latin American Therapeutic Communities.

Established in 1975 in Bangkok, Thailand, the WFTC was initially created as a section of the International Council on Alcohol and Addictions (ICAA) but eventually established itself as its own federation under the leadership of Msgr. William O'Brien, Daytop Village's first president. Since its inception, it has organized world conferences on the TC every two years. Hosted in various countries, these gatherings are attended by drug experts, academics, policy makers, program administrators, and addiction professionals and are venues to share new technologies in drug treatment and the development of TC. Through the years, INL has provided generous funding to several WFTC conferences.

Chapter 2

Cultural Diffusion and Evolution of the Therapeutic Community

The Importance of a Standard Practice

S tandard practice creates a replicable pattern for learning and teaching or practicing the TC concept. It allows us to measure and compare treatment outcomes and it lends to fidelity to the practice of the TC. Even in the U.S., there is a widespread lack of consistency in the practice of the TC method. There is also limited literature that delineates the various TC tools and interventions used in the concept-based TC.

There are three important personalities whose long experience in the practice and development of the concept-based TC has contributed to codifying the TC principles and practice. David Deitch, whose experience reaches as far back as Synanon but later joined Daytop Village, has done his share of expounding on the early TC concepts. His contributions have been penned in numerous scientific papers. He developed elaborate training curricula on the practice of the TC, which became the training bible of Daytop's international training program (Daytop, 1992). However, he has yet to come up with a definitive work that focuses extensively on explaining the TC theories and practices and how to integrate them into current evidence-based practices that address addiction.

Lewis Yablonsky (1965, 1989) also made a huge contribution to the literature on the TC by reporting on the origins and philosophy of the concept-based TC that developed at Synanon (Sadly, he passed away this January, 2014). His classic book, *Synanon: The Tunnel Back*, was an early account of the Synanon Movement but there was still very little covering the "how-to" or clinical techniques of the TC. His books also lacked an in depth and extensive look at the psychological principles involved in the use of the TC tools or methodologies.

George De Leon, who pioneered the research on the TC, assisted in the training and development of TC programs in different agencies both in the U.S. and overseas. He also published the first comprehensive book on the concept-based TC model, *Therapeutic Community: Theory, Model, and Method*, but it was not published until 2000 when the TC was already an established drug treatment model that had been dispersed worldwide.

A good example of the diversity in the interpretations and implementation of the TC philosophy and practices is exemplified by a large drug treatment program in New York. As one of the largest programs in the U.S. with roots in the TC, it has either acquired or merged with several traditional TCs in New York and other states. Although it still uses the TC model in most of its residential programs, it avoids describing the programs as "TCs." Several of its adopted treatment facilities have practiced their own brand of TC for many years and continue to do so even after being absorbed by the corporate program. There is no single TC model or uniform TC practice within the agency. The current use of TC tools and interventions is as varied as the terminologies used to describe them. This case is not unique. This is unfortunately a widespread trend.

Despite the diversity of interpretations of the TC practice, there is consensus in its general principles. For example, the practice of "community-as-method" is universally agreed upon as the TC's keystone principle. This is discussed at length in Chapter 4. Another common principle is the holistic view of addiction and its treatment. The inconsistency begins to appear when these principles are put to practice. Often, although well intentioned TCs are rooted in these principles, their practices do not fully reflect or run counter to the TC principles. The level of experience and expertise of the practitioner can be an important factor in determining the fidelity of the TC implementation. Unfortunately, even with experienced practitioners, the lack of standard guidelines in the practice of the TC results in great variations among drug programs that claim to use the TC. This fact makes it difficult to perform studies that compare the effectiveness of TC with other models.

Hybridization of the Therapeutic Community

The absence of standard guidelines in the practice of the TC has led to the gradual drift away from the original TC concepts and practice principles. The general method for learning and adopting the TC for foreign drug treatment programs usually involves the foreign staff paying visits to American TCs and living in the TC houses as "residents" in a learning-by-doing process. In some cases, especially in the early days of the TC, there was very little formal instruction, supervision, or reference literature provided for interns or trainees. There was no "quality control," so to speak. Trainees went back to their home countries and implemented the TC according to how they understood the concepts. Cultural, social, and professional biases of the person implementing the TC often come into play when setting up a TC. As a result, there is now a myriad of TCs across the globe with limited fidelity to practice. Some still continue to practice antiquated methodologies that are inconsistent with the current model. Figure 2.1 below depicts the hybridization of the TC through cultural diffusion.

Figure 2.1 Hybridization of the TC Through Cultural Diffusion

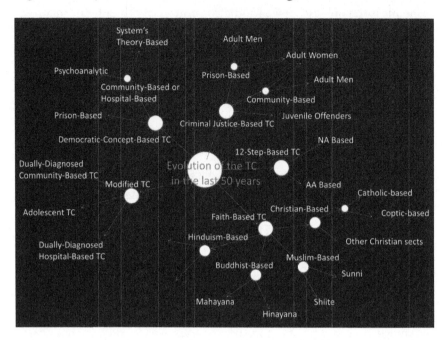

Factors that Contribute to Hybridization

The term "hybridization" is used to describe the transformations of the TC as it was adopted in various places and treatment settings. The term and concept is borrowed from the paleoanthropologist Chris Stringer (2012) which he used to describe the "netlike pattern produced by gene flow between evolutionarily separate lineages . . . (p. 249)." Stringer employed the term to explain the results of interbreeding of ancient species of human's forebears. The concept is used here as an analogy describing the outcome of the marriage between the TC and other ideologies.

Each time the TC is introduced into a new region, its model and concepts undergo cultural transformations driven by several socio-cultural factors. Very often, the personal and professional background of the person who introduces the model to the host country leaves a very distinct mark. For instance, those persons trained in traditional psychology or psychiatry are likely to develop TCs that have strong psychotherapeutic elements. They might combine psychodynamic approaches or incorporate family therapy or system's theory into the TC program. Persons with strong religious background are often attracted to the communal lifestyle of the TC and its ecumenical and universalistic perspective. These preferences or biases can strongly influence the leadership's interpretation of the TC and the way in which it is ultimately adopted and adapted into the host culture.

In the early years of the TC, many Christian religious leaders who founded TCs were often motivated by a strong sense of Christian mission. While there was always a mix of professional and paraprofessional staff in these TCs, the spirit of religious service and sacrifice often prevailed in the work ethic and values of everyone. The same mindset dictated the way in which these organizations conducted business. Making money was secondary and providing treatment services to as many individuals as possible was primary, regardless of religious persuasion or the individual's ability to pay for treatment. It was not unusual for staff to voluntarily work long hours and to believe in the overall goal and mission of the TC. They did what was necessary to help people in need and were prepared to do whatever it took. All these factors contributed to the shaping of the organizational culture, the way in which staff carried out their functions, and ultimately the norms and values of these TCs.

The following are some of the important factors that contribute to the hybridization process. Each factor has contributed to the modification of the original TC model.

Belief System Surrounding Addiction

This refers to a set of beliefs regarding addiction and human behavior such as how a particular culture views addiction. Some cultures, while trying to understand the root causes of addiction, will focus primarily on the drug or chemical, while others will focus on the addict's personal attributes, still others will consider both (Perfas, 2002). When the cause of addiction is attributed to the drug, simple withdrawal from the drug is deemed sufficient treatment. When personality flaws are blamed for addiction, all sorts of "exorcisms" or religious conversions are applied to drive the evil of addiction from the addicted person. These sets of beliefs on the cause of addiction determine the goals of treatment and how change is going to be achieved. This is also true when the Twelve-Step philosophy (used in AA and NA) drives the guiding treatment principles. The result is a hybrid TC with twelve-step underpinnings.

Institutional Goals

When a TC is adopted by an established institution, such as a prison system or a religious group, the overarching goals of that agency will shape how the TC is implemented and practiced. The goal of incarceration is to provide just punishment for an offender's crime against society as well as an opportunity for reforming the offender to avoid recidivism. Often the mission of religious organizations is the salvation of the soul or to provide guidance in how to live a moral life. These institutional goals become an integral part of treatment when the TC is adopted as a treatment model under the auspices of these systems. The norms and values of a religious group, for example, will dictate that faith or religious practices are part of the health and recovery process. How members of the TC relate with each other is also influenced by the norms and values adhered to by the system, including prescriptions for conducting personal affairs. The same argument can be extended to include the influence of a nation as a whole and how its institutions view or interpret addiction.

When addiction is viewed as a "social evil" that corrupts individuals who engage in it, the addict becomes highly stigmatized and treated no differently from a prostitute or a criminal. This perspective shapes the attitude with which society treats the addict and the prescription for curing them. In this case, the TC assumes the role of a social or political reeducation program and incorporates in its practice the social and political policies or agenda of the state. An extension of this perspective is the view of addiction as a public health threat, with potentials for disrupting law and order. With this in mind, the policymaker directs social policy and interventions on the addicted population, whose activities do not only harm themselves but also other members of society.

Harm reduction policy and interventions are designed to minimize the damage inflicted by addiction on the person and the potential harm that the addicted person can cause others. The strategy often has little to do with treating addiction or helping addicts recover.

Culture

The culture of the host country has a major influence in the way the TC concepts are interpreted and put to practice. Cultural beliefs, customs, traditions, and language contribute greatly to the variability of how the TC is practiced. It is through the lens of cultural bias that the TC's own "sub-culture" is adopted by the host country. For example, expressing honest negative or positive feelings directly to peers is standard practice in TC but in some cultures it is frowned upon. Also, chronological age of peers means little in Western TC's, whereas in certain cultures people are accorded with greater respect based on age, seniority, or social standing. Terminologies unique to the TC often have no equivalent in other languages, so something inevitably gets lost in the translation to another culture. Religious beliefs or practices are also sometimes integrated into the TC. In Islamic societies, the required prayers five times a day become part of the TC daily structure. In most religiously inspired TCs, conversion from a life of sin to one of faith is viewed as a necessary part of the change process from addiction to a life of recovery.

Political and Social Infrastructure

The success with which the TC is adopted by a culture or society is determined by both their level of sophistication in the field of drug treatment as well as the existence of appropriate social infrastructure that supports the treatment of addiction. While some countries have achieved technological advances in the development of treatment approaches to addiction, there are still many countries that are unequipped to provide reasonable treatment for addiction. Some resort to wholesale drug substitution/maintenance programs or incarceration as the primary strategy for curbing the problem of addiction and the crimes associated with addiction. Others which have been able to develop an evidence-based biopsychosocial model for treating addiction often offer a mixture of wide-ranging treatment strategies.

In many developing countries, publicly-funded community-based drug treatment services are almost non-existent; if they do exist, they are often an extension of the criminal justice system. Voluntary treatment services are provided by privately owned drug treatment agencies whose fees are often beyond the reach of the common drug addict. Most drug-addicted clients, who are generally poor, often end up incarcerated for crimes committed to support their drug habit. In these countries, the few TCs in prisons are their only means of getting help without having to pay for treatment services. Despite the need for a sustainable drug treatment for the significant population of drug offenders in prisons, there are not enough TC programs in prisons. Moreover, the prison TCs that are in place are not staffed with corrections personnel that are well trained in the TC. Fidelity to the TC principles is severely lacking in these programs, and the highly punitive prison culture often reigns.

Cultural Drift

In the process of the TC's global dispersion, hybridization of the TC model is inevitable. The TC's treatment milieu with its own set of cultural norms and values that are designed to support recovery from addiction is subject to "cultural drift," to borrow Stringer's (2012) terminology, as it finds itself in various host cultures. Not all of the changes are intentional and are often due to misinterpretation or failure to fully understand the original concept. As some of the TC concepts and practices are adapted to fit into the requirements of the new setting or host culture, the changes that take place eventually take hold. Over time, the transplanted TC takes a life of its own, thus forming a hybrid TC.

However, not all forms of hybrid TCs are dysfunctional as there are adaptive cultural drifts and disruptive ones. Some changes made to the TC "culture" and practices remain true to the model and do not undermine its principles. These are called "adaptive changes" and serve to enhance the TC model. There are other changes, however, which not only deviate from the original TC model but also undermine the true spirit of the TC. The following are some characteristics of changes that contribute to either adaptive or disruptive cultural drifts:

- **Adaptive**
  - Changes that are consistent with the basic principles of the TC
  - Changes that enhance the original concept
    - Examples: the reentry & aftercare program, staffing with a mix of ex-addict and professional staff, the structure and phases of the encounter group process, incorporating family therapy and family programs, application of motivational incentives to complement TC privileges, etc.

- **Disruptive**
  - Changes that are inconsistent or in conflict with basic TC principles
  - Changes that are unproductive and ineffective in promoting change
    - Examples: shaming, confrontation that intentionally provokes negative feelings, excessive cursing, excessive use of behavior-shaping tools and minimal use of emotional/psychological tools, punitive use of learning experiences, exploitation of resident labor, use of physically coercive tools (e.g., putting residents on chains or locked rooms), etc.

Chapter 3

The Major Structural Components and Practice Principles of the Therapeutic Community

There are five major structural components of the TC discussed in this model, namely (1) *treatment structure*, (2) *treatment condition*, (3) *staff role and function*, (4) *biopsychosocial treatment interventions*, and (5) *treatment outcome and feedback*. Each component has a set of practice principles. From a social system's perspective, the components are the *structures* which are features representing the underlying order that guide the operational performance of the TC, whereas the practice principles are *functions* representing the actual performance or activities.

Adherence to the TC practice principles is necessary to accomplish what the TC was designed to do. The goal is to create a dynamic and safe therapeutic environment that promotes the process of change within a self-help, social learning context. One should consider these principles to be the necessary ingredients for a successful TC as the application of these principles is what creates a context where "healing" can occur.

The TC has come a long way from its roots in Synanon and the early days of experimenting with harnessing the power of community to shape human behavior, feeling, and thinking. Along the way, it has developed basic treatment principles, which have been honed and refined by succeeding generations of TCs.

The major structural components and practice principles of the TC are a collection of the original TC concepts that remain relevant and consistent with current practices in addiction treatment. Some have been added as the TC has evolved with current best practices in drug treatment and rehabilitation. (A survey instrument designed to evaluate the extent to which these principles are practiced in a TC is provided in the Appendix).

Major Components and Practice Principles

A. Treatment Structure

Treatment structure refers to the social organization of the TC and how treatment activities are organized which is outlined by the following practice principles:

Principle 1 – *There is a progression of treatment through outlined phases*

Treatment in a TC is a developmental process marked by movement through phases or stages. The following *phases*, with minor variations, are followed in TCs all over the world:

- *Orientation/Induction* – The orientation process may be as brief as a week or as long as a month depending on the length of the TC program. In most short-term TCs, which have an average residency of three months, orientation lasts from one to two weeks. In longer programs, orientation is generally between three to four weeks. Orientation, or Induction, is designed to help new residents integrate into the TC by teaching its concepts and practices. It is also the treatment phase where residents learn about the nature of addiction and what is involved in the recovery process. Substance abusers come into treatment with varying levels of motivation and are often driven by external pressures rather than the genuine desire to receive help for their problems or give up substance use. To prevent residents from leaving treatment prematurely, which often happens in this phase, motivational enhancement strategies must be incorporated into the orientation process. The orientation process also provides staff with the opportunity to continue to conduct clinical assessments as new residents adapt to the TC environment.

- *Core Treatment* – This is the treatment phase in which residents are completely immersed into the therapeutic milieu of the TC. In this phase, residents experience various TC processes, including the evidence-based interventions, e.g., *relapse prevention, trauma group, anger management, contingency management therapy,* etc., which are outlined in their individualized treatment plans. Residents perform various job functions and move up the social hierarchy of the community based on their job performance and treatment progress. The job functions, or therapeutic work assignments, assume an important role not only in the maintenance of the community but also as a vehicle for imparting pro-social values.

- *Pre-reentry* – In the pre-reentry phase, residents participate in activities that are relevant to their reintegration back into society, such as learning relapse prevention skills, vocational assessment and training, family counseling/ therapy, monitored home visits, and many others. Social reintegration is a gradual process of re-exposure to society at large which helps to avoid the shock of a sudden loosening of the highly structured social environment of the TC. By the time residents have reached this treatment phase, they usually have high positions in the community. They are part of the "upper" social structure and have assumed leadership roles. In effect, they are role-models in the community.

- **Reentry** – During this phase, residents spend the greater part of their time outside of the TC. Those who need housing are often referred to a reentry house or a halfway house where they can continue to work on their recovery while pursuing various means of supporting themselves. Although the TC remains their main source of social and emotional support, they work on gradually rebuilding their future sources of social support outside of the TC. Community-based social support groups, such as Alcoholics Anonymous, Narcotics Anonymous, and other 12-step based programs, are highly recommended during this stage of treatment.

- **Aftercare** – In this phase, the residents are considered to have completed their formal treatment. However, they can continue to receive help to solidify their recovery or address long-term and on-going issues. For example, they might need continuing mental health or medical assistance, recovery support groups, specialized therapy, or counseling. Residents should already be familiar with the 12-step program by this time.

In each phase, residents are expected to master certain tasks and consistently demonstrate adaptive behaviors and attitudes. The timeline of the individualized treatment plan is developed for each resident in relation to the treatment phases. Each treatment plan, which is designed collaboratively by the resident and staff to meet the resident's specific treatment needs, outlines the goals of each phase. The staff will provide the prescribed interventions and create opportunities for the resident to meet his goals. In turn, the resident is responsible for achieving these goals and pursuing activities that will allow him to realize these goals. The treatment plan is regularly reviewed and revised according to the resident's treatment progress or as new issues or needs arise.

Setting measurable treatment goals and objectives, in tandem with criteria for moving up through the treatment phases, creates a framework that delineates when it is appropriate for residents to advance through the phases. A treatment plan-driven treatment process through the TC phases repudiates the argument that the TC approach is "one treatment fits all" and ignores individual needs.

The major challenge facing the TC practitioner in implementing a treatment plan-driven process is how TC processes are used to help residents meet treatment needs and achieve their treatment goals and objectives. For example, how assigning a resident a particular job function might help him develop social skills or overcome personal inadequacies. A resident who suffers from a stage fright might be asked to have a small role in a morning meeting. The staff or counselor must have a thorough knowledge of each resident's background and treatment plan for this process to work well.

Principle 2 – There is a process for joining the community that explores treatment motivation and promotes "belongingness"

To become part of TC, prospective residents participate in an entry interview process conducted by senior peers. Not to be confused with the formal intake interview, which is conducted for the purpose of screening and assessment, this introductory interview serves the purpose of helping prospective residents examine their own motivation for joining the TC and setting the tone of what treatment in the TC will look like if they are accepted. New residents often have mixed feelings about coming into treatment and their real intentions can be overshadowed by pressures from family, the court, probation/parole officers, or an employer. It's not uncommon for prospective residents to have multiple sources of external pressures forcing them to seek help. As a result, during this peer-conducted interview process, they may be angry and defiant or may simply have no clear reasons of their own as to why they should join the TC for treatment. The interview gives them a chance to separate other people's expectations from their own feelings about the nature of their problems, and is a first step in revealing how they can begin to take some control of what happens next. This process helps the interviewers get an idea of the level of motivation of prospective residents and how to help them examine their conflicting feelings about the need for help. This process also helps prospective residents gain clarity on the choices they have, making it easier for them to examine their motivation for treatment and understand the need to take responsibility for it, vis-à-vis the demands from the court, family, or employers.

The entry interview also provides the opportunity for prospective residents to interact with people who have been through experiences similar to their own and relate with them not as authority figures but as "peers." In this kind of social interaction, it becomes much easier for prospective residents to drop their defenses and façade and respond to questions more honestly than if they were responding to, say, the police or a counselor. This process also shows how amenable they would be to constructive suggestions and expectations of the TC if they are admitted.

If a prospective resident is accepted into the TC at the completion of the entry interview, he should already feel a sense of belonging, especially once he is introduced to his "big brother" (or sister, if a female). His big brother will act as a peer-mentor, helping him navigate the first few weeks of his residency while the risk of dropping out of treatment early is high. To minimize the chances of leaving treatment prematurely, residents must be provided with support and guidance by their peers, in addition to engagement strategies and motivational counseling from staff. In drawing from surveys of TC residents concerning factors that helped them adjust to the TC environment, the influence of big brothers and sisters has been shown to be quite significant.

In short, the goal of the second TC principle is to help new residents understand and build upon their motivation for treatment, promote belongingness, establish personal responsibility for treatment or change, and confirm their treatment fitness for the TC. In a study by Pearce and Pickard (2012), they found two factors that when combined enhance a TC's effectiveness. These factors are the *promotion of belongingness* and the *capacity for personal responsibility*, which are uniquely emphasized in the TC. A sense of belongingness is important to "buying-into" the TC process and is also significantly correlated with better self-esteem. Baumeister and Leary (1995) argue that in order for "belongingness" to be meaningful contact between members of the community must: (1)

be frequent, (2) be pleasant and satisfying, (3) be stable over time, and (4) include the presence of positive feelings of mutual concern.

The focus on encouraging prospective residents to take responsibility for their treatment in the entry interview is based on the assumption that if they are able to achieve this, they are more likely to engage in behavior change. A cognitive shift in a prospective resident's causal attribution of his problem, from one that puts the blame on others to one that holds himself accountable, must happen during the interview in order for change to begin to be possible. His willingness to engage in behavioral change is associated with his ability to take responsibility for his problem and for finding its solution.

Principle 3 – *There is an orientation process that educates, engages, and facilitates new resident's integration into the community*

To assist new residents in adjusting and integrating into the community, they must undergo an orientation process about the TC program following admission. This process involves learning the TC philosophy and concepts, such as organizational structure, job functions, TC treatment tools, group processes and meetings, and activities and rituals of the community. Since residents are expected to get involved and actively participate in program or community activities, an effective system of orientation is necessary to prepare them to cope with the demands of the community. Understanding how the TC works and what roles its members play is crucial in getting new residents engaged in treatment as soon as they join the community.

During orientation, the norms and rules of the community are discussed in depth. Residents are taught about the rules and the consequences for failing to follow them. While it is essential to emphasize the importance of rules in maintaining safety and preserving the integrity of the community, efforts should be made to explain how these rules connect to the individual resident's personal goal of recovery. It would be difficult to achieve the goal of recovery or change within a chaotic or unsafe environment, but it is equally important that residents make the connection between the community rules and how these facilitate the achievement of their goal of recovery. For members of a treatment population who are not used to following rules and are notorious for defying regulations, they are likely to find the TC norms and rules highly restrictive. To prevent *psychological reactance* (Brehm, 1966), or attempts to sabotage the established order of the community, an effective strategy is needed to help them invest in the community rules.

While residents are undergoing the orientation process, they should start being exposed to processes that help them learn and understand basic information about "feelings and emotions" in preparation for group processes, such as "conflict resolution," "anger management," "loss and bereavement," and relapse prevention," to mention a few. These are processes that they will undergo later in treatment and require that they have the ability to self-disclose and be able to identify, process, and articulate feelings and emotions. The orientation process should assist new residents in achieving a sufficient amount of emotional stability before they are exposed to traditional TC group processes and evidence-based groups. The benefits from these group processes are enhanced by each resident's emotional readiness to engage in treatment.

Counselors are assigned to new residents during the orientation process and should immediately get them engaged through motivational counseling, as well as help them cope with the challenges of adapting to life in the community. In studies, the quality of the counselor-client relationship has been found to be a significant factor in client treatment retention and effective outcome (Belding, et al., 1997; Joe, et al., 2001; Simpson, 2004). Developing strong and positive counselor relationships with residents increases the potential for keeping new residents in the TC for the duration of treatment.

Principle 4 – *There is a process for separating from the community*
When a resident decides to leave treatment against clinical advice, efforts should be made to dissuade him through counseling by his peers and staff. If all means have been exhausted to try to keep him in treatment and he still insists on leaving, there is a discharge process that must be followed.

A discharge plan must be put together that includes a referral to another agency or, at the very least, he must be provided with the addresses and contact numbers of appropriate agencies whose services he might need. The safety of the resident is an important consideration when he leaves the community, and in the case of a minor, the family or guardian must be informed of his decision to leave and transportation with the family should be arranged.

When a resident is adamant about leaving the TC prematurely without good reasons, he often creates negative feelings within the community. Some of his peers, including staff, sometimes feel betrayed, especially when time and energy have been spent trying to help the person cope with his early struggles within the community. Negative feelings aside, the resident must be made to feel that the option to return to the community is always available, except when the resident has demonstrated behavior deemed inappropriate for treatment in a TC.

Program separation through completion or graduation, on the other hand, is an occasion for celebration. Upon completion of treatment, residents embark on rebuilding their lives and continuing recovery. After a significant amount of time has lapsed, a graduation ceremony is held to recognize those who were able to maintain their sobriety and live productive lives. However, graduation or completion is not the end of the connection between the resident and the TC. During treatment a lifetime of relationship is forged, and graduates are always welcome to visit and spend time to "give back" to the TC as role-models to new members. Graduates who demonstrate clinical or counseling skills and who are interested in a career in the helping profession often continue their training to become TC staff.

Principle 5 – *Community members are organized into a social hierarchy with a structure of responsibilities*

Figure 3.1 illustrates the organizational structure of the TC or the "chain of command" through which communication from the bottom of the hierarchy moves up and directives from above flow down. Each community member has a role and function according to his status or position in the hierarchy.

Figure 3.1 The Social Hierarchy of the TC

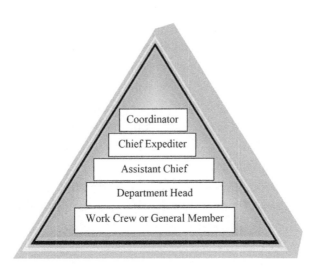

Occupying the top positions are senior residents who earn these positions according to their time in treatment, treatment progress, and demonstrated knowledge and skills of the TC processes. They are considered the "role- models" of the community whom younger members look up to as leaders, and they keep their positions provided they continue to be role-models and dependable community leaders who lead the TC in a way that promotes recovery. Any indications of deviation from the norms and values of the community or involvement in misconduct will cause senior residents to lose their status or positions immediately.

Underneath the senior residents are the general residents who comprise the workforce of various departments. There is regular reshuffling of job positions in the community, and those who fail to live up to expected behavioral standards are immediately demoted or lose their positions in the next rounds of job changes. In this way, all residents have the opportunity to move up the ladder, and those demoted can always redeem themselves by working on earning their status back through consistent good behavior.

In this system, there are clear lines of responsibilities which make it easier for residents to be held accountable in the conduct of their therapeutic work assignments or duties. When this system is properly implemented, the TC functions like a well-oiled machine and an effective vehicle for empowering the residents and imparting social responsibility. By using this social system, the residents learn to follow rules, appreciate the value of work and responsibility, and acquire pro-social values necessary to succeed in the "world of work."

B. Treatment Condition

Treatment condition refers to the qualitative requirements necessary to establish a healthy TC environment. This is accomplished by adhering to the following practice principles:

Principle 1 – *Safety is foremost*

Safety is a necessary condition for facilitating positive change. The treatment environment should be both physically and emotionally safe to encourage self-disclosure and to promote self-help as well as mutual help among community members. This principle has received a significant amount of attention in recent years as research studies on trauma and Post Traumatic Stress Disorder (PTSD) consistently indicate that a significant number of substance abusers have experienced trauma in one form or another. In clinical substance use disorder samples, the prevalence of lifetime PTSD ranges from 26 to 52% (Mills, et al., 2005; Dom, et al., 2007) and for current PTSD the range is 15-41% (Reynolds, et al., 2005; Clark, et al., 2001). In general, substance abusers who have experienced trauma or PTSD, especially those with complex trauma, do not do well in treatment and are likely to drop-out before completion of treatment. The feeling of safety is of paramount importance for this treatment population. They often present complex treatment issues, and when exposed to a threatening or unsafe environment, they can manifest trauma symptoms that are disruptive to the community (Bloom, 1997; Najavits, 2002).

TCs should have clear admission criteria and effective screening processes to weed out those for whom treatment in a TC is not appropriate. Applicants with severe mental illness and those with serious histories of violent behavior are often denied admission for safety reasons. The TC has a set of "cardinal rules" and "house rules" which forbid acts or threats of violence, drug use, and sexual acting out. These are designed to protect and promote the safety of the community, and residents are required to swear to abide by them.

There are also surveillance procedures in place in each TC that control and track down residents' movements in and outside of the community. Part of the functions of the TC organizational structure is to regularly monitor residents' activities and whereabouts.

Principle 2 – *The treatment process must be dynamic and pervasive*
An important characteristic of treatment in a TC is the element of challenge. This is accomplished through the constant demands placed on residents to be vigilant and aware of both internal, or psychological, processes and the external group dynamics of the community. Everyone is expected to take "pride in quality" in all aspects of community life which is reflected in how one accomplishes tasks or conducts himself. In order to sustain residents' motivation and interest, the treatment process must be dynamic and the spirit of "community" must permeate the treatment environment. Given this context, the community is able to facilitate the change process; and learning opportunities, provided through social interaction and feedback from members, are maximized.

In the spirit of "responsible concern," the use of TC tools such as confronting, pulling-up, pushing-up, providing feedback, relating (sharing one's negative or positive feelings) are part of routine practice of TC residents. These therapeutic processes are essential in effecting behavioral and attitudinal shifts among residents, and are a means of establishing and maintaining the values and norms of the TC, as well as creating a dynamic community that is alive and vibrant.

The daily schedule must reflect this dynamic and pervasive nature of treatment in the TC. Although some activities are routine, novelty and challenge are maintained by setting and resetting the treatment thermostat in response to community issues that frequently arise. For example, community sanctions, or "bans," might be imposed to part of or the entire community for flagrant violations of house rules. On the contrary, a community outing may be planned as a reward for outstanding achievement by the community.

Ensuring a dynamic and pervasive treatment process is necessary to create the therapeutic dosage and salience required to impact entrenched addictive habits, reshape attitudes and behaviors associated with a substance abuse lifestyle, and shift cognitive thinking patterns associated with an addictive mentality (Perfas, 2012).

Principle 3 – *The TC is a peer-driven treatment process that emphasizes personal responsibility*

The heart of the TC treatment approach is held in the community of peers who hold each other and themselves accountable for their share in the community and for living up to its standards. In the TC, personal responsibility is paramount theme in day-to-day resident conduct, performance of duties in groups and meetings, and in the pursuit of recovery from addiction. This is consistent with the TC's belief that an addicted person must learn to take full responsibility of his problem and getting help to fully benefit from treatment and achieve lasting sobriety. TC residents are fully cognizant and expected to remind each other of this expectation and resist placing blame in others for their own faults or failures. Although many residents are initially resistant to treatment and avoid taking responsibility for them coming to treatment, as they become immersed into the TC, it is expected that their growing awareness and insight will eventually lead them to a better grasp of reality.

Although staff members contribute to reminding residents of the TC's expectations and holding them accountable for their actions, there is no substitute for peer intervention when it comes to dealing with behaviors or attitudes that run counter to community rules and values. The element of identification is powerful among residents, who often share similar histories and difficulties, which makes it easier for them to keep an open mind and be receptive to their peers. The highly peer-driven processes of the TC and the voice that residents exercise in the affairs of the community are not only empowering but also contribute to treatment motivation.

Principle 4 – *The treatment process promotes a culture of self-help and mutual help*

This important principle is closely related to the previous principle and sets the TC apart from other treatment models while linking it to its root, the twelve-step model. Both models share the belief that as a recovering person engages in helping other people, his belief in the possibility of his own recovery is reinforced. The concept of sobriety becomes a living, breathing reality as residents see themselves reflected in other residents who are going through the same struggles while pursuing a similar goal and purpose. The TC, however, takes this to the next level.

While helping their peers, it is not only important for residents to listen carefully. It is equally important to give an honest feedback whether solicited or not. Through "confrontation" their peers help to clarify and raise each other's awareness of aspects of self or reality that might otherwise be ignored or denied. This honest, down-to-earth exchange, done in groups or one-on-one, can be disconcerting to both the giver and the receiver. Nonetheless, residents are expected to tell each other the truth without malice, no matter how unpleasant, in the spirit of "responsible concern." While it is important to give each other an honest feedback, it is equally important for residents to provide each other with emotional support, which may be especially necessary when a resident is in distress. This is the true meaning of self-help and mutual help and how the dual role of a TC resident as "client-therapist" is operationalized.

Principle 5 – *There are shared community norms and values that guide residents' personal conduct*

One may look at the TC as a microcosm of society with its own set of pro-social values and norms. These values are embedded in the TC philosophy, slogans and sayings, the belief system, rules and regulations, and the code of conduct. These are the ingredients of "right living" (De Leon, 2000). Residents are constantly reminded to observe community rules and live by the norms and values of the community. The norms and values are very similar to what most families would teach and expect from their children. The only difference is that the TC amplifies the learning and practice of these norms and values to remind those who knew them before addiction took over their lives, and inculcate them into those who never had the opportunity to learn them before the streets became their training ground.

Sometimes the TC is referred to as the "school of life" because of the behavioral, affective, cognitive, vocational, moral, and social learning experiences it provides. Residents who spend a meaningful amount of time and complete treatment in a TC often are able to cope better with the daily demands of life, work, family, and society as a whole. Those who are able to internalize the TC values and community norms adjust to societal rules and mainstream values much easier than those who never experience a deep connection to the TC. It is important to train residents to follow rules, develop healthy internal structure and discipline, practice compassion, and work with others collaboratively as these are essential in their re-integration into society. A person who is able to relate and identify with societal rules, mores, traditions, and way of life is less inclined to break the law and act-out sociopathic inclinations; whereas, a lost soul who finds himself alienated from society will find it easier to act on his alienation, either by lashing out against societal rules or withdrawing into his own world.

C. Staff Role and Function

This major component provides the guidelines to how staff contributes to the formation of the TC environment and maintenance of its operations. It defines staff's unique role and function in the TC. The following are the practice principles included under this component:

Principle 1 – *The staffing pattern follows a trans-disciplinary model*
In the early days of the TC, most clinical staff were ex-addicts who had undergone treatment in a therapeutic community. Much has changed since then, and there has been a shift to a mix of ex-addict TC graduates and academically-trained staff working side by side in most TCs. While the professional staff bring a different perspective, they do not have the kind of first-hand experience of the TC that ex-addict staff have. Their academic background in the medical field and the social sciences and the ex-addict staff's strong experiential background in treatment can combine to complement each other. However, bringing them to work together effectively as a team is often a challenge, as their training backgrounds and work style can be very different. The task for the academically trained staff is learning and mastering the TC practices. The ex-addict staff already has a thorough understanding of the TC but must work to learn the language of mental health to articulate their understanding of addiction, addictive disorders, and treatment within the academic framework. Figure 3.2 below illustrates this staffing model.

Figure 3.2 Trans-disciplinary Staff Model

While the TC trained ex-addict staff is attuned to the concept of teamwork and the "trans-disciplinary" staffing pattern, professionals who are trained in multi-disciplinary or inter-disciplinary model might find it hard to espouse the TC model and operate within its framework. Besides contributing their expertise to operating a TC and managing cases, members of the trans-disciplinary team must operate within the context of the TC. To do this, staff members must share pertinent information among themselves about cases that may impact the community dynamics. Although clinical staff manages their own individual case-loads, they handle them quite differently than they would in a private practice. Client information otherwise considered confidential might have to be shared with some members of the staff when it pertains to the safety and integrity of the community (e.g., drug use, acts of violence, and other unsafe behaviors). Affiliation with and faith in the TC model are required of team members, a prerequisite that does not necessarily exist in other team models.

The TC provides an overarching structure that organizes and defines staff roles, job functions, and responsibilities. Although professional staff is expected to provide expertise in their chosen field when needed, they function foremost as TC staff and should be willing to step out of their traditional roles when called for. For example, they should know what a *Morning Meeting* is and be able to facilitate one when necessary. They should be familiar with the *Seminar* or the *Encounter Group* and be comfortable conducting either. In their role as TC staff, their job functions and responsibilities usually overlap with those of other TC staff. This can create some amount of ambiguity which might be difficult for some to tolerate. On the other hand, the trans-disciplinary model promotes collaboration and provides the opportunity for continual peer-education between staff members.

Principle 2 – TC staff members carryout their roles and functions as role-models and rational authority

Most drug-addicted persons have major issues with authority figures. Their experiences with abusive or negligent caregivers or harsh encounters with law enforcement have often made them disdainful of authority. For this reason, mistrust of people with authority becomes almost second nature for many of them. It becomes part of their survival strategy while they run the streets. Many of them have very few people they can claim as positive influences in their lives. Their role models often are people who themselves have dysfunctional lives, or for the criminal-addict, those who hold power and influence in the violent world of drugs and crime.

When addicted persons first join the TC, they continue to harbor mistrust towards authority. This posture and attitude takes time to change. While in the TC they must consistently observe that power and authority are earned through good conduct and a show of concern for others. They must perceive the staff and senior residents as role models who exercise authority with transparency. They must dissociate authority with the indifferent, cold, and uncaring powerful figures of their past. TC authority figures must exercise their authority and deal with behavioral issues with care, consistency, fairness, and firmness. The concept of "rational authority" (Brill & Lieberman, 1969) is the creative use of power in a humane and constructive manner to further the cause of rehabilitating the drug-addicted person. For example, a judge might give a drug offender a chance to get help by referring him to a treatment center, instead of throwing the books at him by sending him to jail.

Principle 3 – To operationalize the concept of "community as method," staff must function at three levels of operation: the community level, the individual resident level, and the internal level of feelings and emotions

What sets the TC apart from other treatment models is the concept of community as the source of healing. While traditional mental health models rely on professionals as the treatment experts and the source of therapy, the TC relies on community dynamics as the greatest contributor to therapy. To utilize the power of community to influence behavioral, emotional, attitudinal, and cognitive change, a TC environment must be created. According to Woodhams (2001), this therapeutic environment emerges partly as a function of staff operating at three levels. These levels are the *community level*, the *individual resident level*, and the *internal level of feelings and emotions.*

While operating at the community level, staff members take a global perspective of the community by continually assessing group or community dynamics to ensure that residents utilize the social structure to contribute their share and meet their needs. They are also responsible for assessing and sustaining the integrity of the resident social structure and maintaining the fidelity of the TC practice. At this level staff members support and maintain the TC social system. For example, incidents involving program rule violations are handled by staff not only as problems of the offenders but also as issues that concern the entire community.

When residents approach staff for certain needs or requests, they must first go through the resident social hierarchy (or structure) and account why they should be granted a request to, say, call home or receive a visitor. In this operational level, it is the role of staff to provide support, guidance, and supervision of the TC social hierarchy. This operational function, which is also referred to as "TC Operations," is unique to the TC and often not easily grasped by professionals who are not experientially trained in the TC.

Operating at the level of the individual resident involves knowing residents on a personal basis, familiarity with their treatment issues, and treatment progress. Staff must look at resident behavior in the context of the community by considering how each resident is affected and in turn will affect the community. This also involves an understanding of how interventions directed at a resident will impact him and the community. While staff members keep their focus on the community and the constantly shifting group dynamics, they are ever mindful of each resident's needs, role, function, and performance. In this way, staff roles can be likened to conducting a symphony orchestra in which the conductor hears the totality of the music and is yet able to distinguish the sound of each instrument. This function can also be referred to as "Case Management."

Operating at the level of feelings and emotions requires the TC staff to be aware of the feelings and emotions that can be triggered by their interactions with residents and other staff or events that take place in the community. In a dynamic system such as the TC, where staff members help residents in grappling with difficult and intimate issues, in addition to other challenges involved in performing their job functions, the environment is emotionally charged. The intimacy that grows out of the personal encounters of the TC provokes both positive and negative transferential emotions among residents and staff. The emotional investment necessary for staff to be effective, through the capacity for empathy and compassion, and the responsiveness needed to meet residents' emotional needs can take their toll. Some of the hazards of TC work include over-identification by ex-addict staff with residents, over-compensation by professional staff in dealing with experienced and street-smart residents, and vicarious traumatization. Lack of emotional stability or limited experience in recovery in both recovering and professional staff can put them at risk of burnout or misconduct. Due to the nature of the work and the human tragedies that are often involved in addiction, staff must maintain a high level of awareness of their inner or emotional processes that are triggered by their personal interactions with residents and other staff.

The ability of staff members to harness available emotional support from colleagues and friends, as well as remain receptive to constructive input from professional supervision, will go a long way in helping to maintain their mental health. This important function is related to "Supervision."

Principle 4 – *There is a system for training and supervising the different levels of the residents' social hierarchy*

One of the functions of staff is to supervise the resident social hierarchy and ensure that the senior residents are engaged in training and supervising their work crews. It is through this process that the TC is able to train capable residents and operate a community that is largely maintained by its members. While staff is engaged in the task of running the clinical and administrative aspects of treatment, the residents take a major role in implementing the daily schedule and carrying out community tasks, such as help cook meals, do light maintenance, keep the surroundings clean, etc. Some senior residents who have been through various positions in the hierarchy and possess some clinical or administrative abilities function as junior staff. They are utilized in counseling and advising other residents, facilitating some group processes, and as instructors to assist various work departments to manage work more efficiently.

To manage work in each department more effectively, there is a daily departmental meeting to chart out the tasks for the day. In these meetings, the department heads dole out work assignments and provide feedback to the work crews. A weekly meeting of all departments convened by staff is held to get feedback and assess the progress of the work crews. In these meetings recommendations for promotions, demotions, or work rotations are submitted and discussed. Applications by work crews and recommendations by department heads for privileges, such as home passes or a trip to the mall, are also reviewed for final decision by staff at these meetings.

Sometimes department heads will call for a special encounter group in their departments to iron out differences among crew members. Likewise, staff may organize an encounter group among members of the senior resident hierarchy to settle interpersonal conflict, delineate work responsibilities, or hold accountable those who are not living up to expectations.

Staff supervision of the social hierarchy is crucial in maintaining the standards of the TC and fidelity to the TC practice. Through supervision staff is able to provide the necessary clinical input and train senior residents to assist in the effective management of the resident population and prevention of corruption of the TC social structure.

D. Biopsychosocial Treatment Interventions

This component outlines distinct but overlapping sets of interventions that address the physical, psychological, cognitive, moral, vocational, and social domains of treatment. It includes the following practice principles:

Principle 1 – *There is a set of behavior-shaping strategies and a system of sanctions on "deviant behaviors"*

Figure 3.3 Hierarchy of Behavior Shaping Tools

HIERARCHY OF BEHAVIOR SHAPING TOOLS

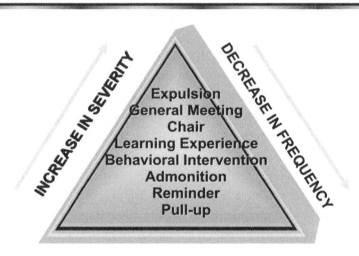

Figure 3.3 above illustrates the hierarchy of the TC behavior-shaping tools. To address serious misconduct the TC has a set of behavior-shaping tools it employs in graduated levels depending on the severity and chronic nature of the behavior it is trying to reprogram. Some of these interventions are designed to reinforce community norms and expectations, while others are means of preventing the escalation of negative behaviors. While application is supervised by staff, most of these interventions, such as the peer intervention, admonition, reminder, and pull-up, involve peers. To avoid the misuse and abuse of these tools, there is a set procedure that residents must follow when using them on behalf of a peer. When deemed appropriate, and depending on the nature of the offense, peers can recommend to staff a learning experience or "sanction" imposed on an offending resident. To use the tools and apply sanctions to address behavioral issues residents must first acquire staff approval.

Much thought is involved in the use of the tools. The target behavior must be put into context, which requires a review of factors such as the offending resident's treatment progress, his mental or psychological status, his major treatment issues, his community status, and the chronic nature of the behavior. All of these factors are taken into account in order to deliver the appropriate corrective action and assess the potential benefits to the resident. The immediate concern is the effective delivery of the peer intervention and how well it will communicate its intended message to the offender and obtain his concrete commitment for correcting his behavior.

The risk of harming the resident more than helping him is foremost in the minds of the staff and the resident team. The delivery of the intervention must follow strict rules. It must address the resident with respect, focus on his behavior more than his personality, communicate concern, provide emotional support after the behavioral intervention, and arouse feelings of guilt without shaming.

The literature on self-conscious or social emotions (Tangney & Dearing, 2002) has been very helpful in shedding light on the effects of the arousal of guilt versus shame in individuals. While it is common to arouse feelings of guilt or shame when implementing behavioral interventions like those used in a TC, the closely related emotions can have very different effects. Guilt arousal tends to elicit corrective behavior as it causes the person to examine his behavior as a failure to live up to social standards and is more likely to precipitate pro-social behavior; whereas, shame arousal is often the result of an assault on the person's self-esteem which can elicit the negative emotions of anger, hostility, denial, and withdrawal. Therefore, for an intervention to have a productive outcome, it must aim to provoke guilt and avoid evoking feelings of shame. Focusing on the individual's behavior as a failure to live up to community standards as opposed to a symptom of a personality defect or other stigmatizing attributes, must be emphasized during behavioral interventions.

More detailed discussion on the theory and practice of the TC behavior-shaping tools is discussed in *Deconstructing the Therapeutic Community* by Fernando Perfas (2012).

Principle 2 – *There is a structured reward system of privileges and motivational incentives*

Earning privileges in the TC serves a larger purpose than simply rewarding positive behavior. It is a means of inculcating values, such as the importance of working for what a person wants and learning to delay gratification. Earned privileges are structured according to the length of time in treatment and the meeting of behavioral criteria.

The following are three types of privileges in the TC which residents earn as they progress in treatment (Perfas, 2012):

General Privileges are those that are gradually earned by new residents as they make progress in treatment and show consistent good behavior. Some examples of these privileges are permission to make phone calls home, write letters, make a request for a group outing, or trip to the mall.

Status Privileges are privileges that come with positions of responsibility, such as giving seminars, facilitating group activities, running outside errands for the community, or permission to have "walking around money" (WAM).

Reentry Privileges are granted to senior residents who are on their way to returning home. For example, reentry residents may apply for school or job privileges outside of the TC, spend more time at home, or drive a personal car.

Privileges are earned and granted on a "deserving basis" and can be withdrawn or suspended due to program rule violations or relapse to substance use. For example, a department head who is demoted for poor behavior also loses the privileges attached to his position until he is able to earn his status back.

Another set of rewards, which are not contingent on length of time in treatment but instead are used to jump start treatment motivation, are those which are part of "contingency management" or "motivational incentives" (Higgins & Petry, 1999; Petry, 2000; Rowan-Szal, et al.,2000). This set of rewards is used to reinforce positive or productive behaviors as they occur in new members of the community. The rewards are immediate and target behaviors that facilitate program engagement or affiliation to the community. Contingency management complements the TC privileges, especially in the early phases of treatment. The rewards can be as simple as a "push-up" during morning meeting, an in-house movie pass, or earning redeemable points for snacks (Perfas, 2012).

The use of behavior-shaping tools to address misconduct is an essential component of the TC approach. However, they must be balanced with the use of rewards and motivational incentives to reshape unproductive behaviors and enhance motivation for change.

Principle 3 – *Medical and mental health services are available to assess, intervene, and monitor medical and psychiatric conditions that co-occur with substance abuse*

In a national survey by Substance Abuse and Mental Health Services Administration (SAMHSA, 2010), it was reported that 42.8 percent (8.9 million) of adults with substance use disorders had co-occurring mental illness. Studies have shown that more than 50% of substance abuse clients in drug treatment programs suffer from a co-occurring psychiatric disorder in addition to their substance abuse problems. Within this group are clients who have experienced severe or chronic trauma who are not responsive to traditional treatment approaches. To determine if potential residents with this profile are appropriate for treatment in a traditional TC, it is necessary to consider some of the TC approaches that may have iatrogenic effect or unintended consequences on them.

To benefit from the TC experience, it is essential that a resident is able to integrate into the community and function adequately. If a resident suffers from acute cognitive and affective deficits due to severe mental illness, he might find it difficult to adapt to the rigors of treatment. In this case, it may be best to find an alternative program such as a modified TC to meet his particular needs. Residents whose mental health disorders respond to psychiatric medications that stabilize their moods or other cognitive deficits often thrive well in a regular TC. This is only possible when there is regular assessment of their condition and monitoring of their medications by medical and psychiatric staff and close collaborations with the TC counseling staff (Perfas & Spross, 2007).

There are several treatment issues that arise when treating the dual problems of drug abuse and mental illness as both conditions interact in reciprocal ways, such that a relapse in one leads to relapse in the other. In these cases it is most logical to adopt an integrated model of treatment for substance abuse and mental health problems. The simultaneous treatment of both conditions requires widening the scope of treatment to include issues such as the education of residents about medications, medication effects, and side-effect management; behavioral issues surrounding medication compliance; calibrating interventions according to the client's mental status; and the stigma attached to mental illness. Residents' medication non-compliant behavior is often related to ignorance of how medications work, managing side-effects, and understanding the nature of co-occurring disorders. Due to widespread ignorance of residents who suffer from the condition and their peers about co-occurring disorders and psychiatric treatment, most residents hide their disorder for fear of being stigmatized as mentally ill. These are legitimate issues that concern the entire community and must be addressed in groups and meetings using peers and the community to weigh in on the issues (Perfas & Spross, 2007).

Substance abusers, especially those with long-term, chronic use history, often present a variety of medical conditions that are either related to or aggravated by substance abuse. Very often their medical symptoms are masked by their substance abuse and their health conditions come to light only when all forms of substance use cease. It's not uncommon that medical problems begin to trouble a newly recovering person in addition to the physical and psychological pain associated with drug abuse cessation. Staff should be able to determine the gravity, level of priority, and response to each resident's case. Most TCs are staffed with medical personnel who are able to respond to minor medical issues. However, serious medical emergencies are often referred to outside medical providers.

Principle 4 – *Community members are provided with interventions and activities that help resolve psychological problems and promote emotional growth*

While the behavior-shaping tools are designed to correct misguided behavior and produce immediate results, interventions that target emotional issues or unresolved emotional conflicts may require a sustained process, such as on-going individual counseling or group therapy. The TC has traditional group processes that are designed to assist residents in coming to terms with life-long issues and develop a deeper understanding of how these issues have contributed to their substance abuse and other difficulties.

The *probe* (an eight to ten hours sessions of continuous group process focused on a particular theme) and the *marathon* (a non-stop group process that lasts between forty-eight to seventy-two hours) are homegrown group therapies that were popular during the early days of the TC. These group processes were effective in meeting the psychological needs of residents but have disappeared in most modern TCs. They were given up because they were labor-intensive and demanded time and expertise from the dwindling number of traditionally-trained TC staff. Moreover, there were very few conclusive research studies that were conducted to test their efficacy and support their practice as evidence-based, although there were many anecdotal materials from former TC residents that attested to their usefulness. However, research studies performed over the last decade regarding Attachment Theory have provided good reasons to revisit the classic TC groups. Many of the studies provided support for the rationale, goals, and primary focus of the TC's traditional group processes. By grounding these group processes on attachment theory, they can be resurrected and made more evidence-based.

Individual counseling, which is often conducted informally, is focused on correcting specific behaviors relevant to the "here and now." With the influx of mental health staff trained in traditional counseling practices, counseling in the TC has acquired a more formal character of psychotherapy. The same can be said for group therapy. With the increased popularity of evidence-based group therapies, the traditional TC group therapies have been supplanted by groups that focus on issues such as *relapse prevention, anger management, criminal thinking, trauma,* and other *psycho-education issues.* The TC practitioner should be able to seamlessly integrate these groups within the TC treatment framework while maintaining fidelity to both practices.

There are also group therapies that follow specific models such as *cognitive behavioral therapy, dialectical behavior therapy, or seeking safety,* which are designed for residents who present a particular co-occurring condition that must be treated concurrently. The infusion of science-based practices into the psychological interventions of the TC has had an enriching influence on the TC's repertoire of treatment interventions. What has caused confusion is the lack of understanding by some practitioners that these interventions must occur within the context of the TC, not a substitute or separate form of treatment, but as enhancements to the TC therapeutic system.

In the Synanon model, the behavioral and psychological approaches for changing behavior were not clearly delineated. They overlapped, as is the case in most of the more popular TC interventions. For example, the *encounter group* (a group that focuses on raising awareness of discordant behaviors and resolving interpersonal conflict) can be considered both a behavior-shaping and psychological tool. It is a group process but not necessarily considered a form of group therapy, although it has all its elements. The same can be said about the *morning meeting* (a daily community gathering dedicated to building community spirit) which falls under the category of TC meetings; however it has also elements of the *behavior shaping tools.*

Principle 5 – *The community provides interventions and activities that enhance intellectual abilities, self-awareness, moral reasoning, and self-actualization*

The psychosocial development of residents in a TC and the process of internalization of treatment follow Maslow's (1954) hierarchy of needs which is outlined in Figure 3.4.

Figure 3.4 Maslow's Hierarchy of Needs

As new residents become comfortable in the TC environment and feel able to meet their physical survival needs, they will begin to "test the waters" of treatment. They want to know if they can let their guard down, feel physically and psychologically safe in expressing them-selves and participating in activities, and give feedback without fear of retribution. Once they have settled into the TC routine, they begin to feel integrated into the community and develop closeness and intimacy with their peers. The next step is to aspire for greater affiliation to their new found "family" by seeking responsible positions and social recognition from their peers through different job positions. They will start to aspire towards achieving social status in the community. As they acquire more "clean time under their belts" and continue to work on their sobriety, they begin to look for greater meaning and purpose beyond recovery. They might imagine what life will look like in the aftermath of treatment or contemplate a meaningful career.

The most popular outlet or avenue for expressing creative ideas is the seminar, which takes place daily in the TC. The seminar is used as the main tool for disseminating information about new policies or imparting practical knowledge and skills. Topics such as human emotions, dealing with stress, honesty, responsibility, and smoking cessation, among others, are discussed and elaborated upon in these practical, down to earth exchanges that often connect the topics to life in the TC. The seminars, which are often conducted in a participative and interactive style, encourage and train residents to articulate their ideas in a more systematic fashion. Seminars conducted in a "debate" format – with topics such as "Religion versus Spirituality" or "Is Work Gender Related?"–are excellent exercises for residents to take and argue a position. Some seminars involve complex subject matter delivered by an expert speaker in one presentation or in a series of seminars. The exposure to a wide variety of topics and the opportunity to articulate one's ideas and examine opposing ideas and perspectives help expand the residents' breadth of understanding.

In addition to the seminar there are a variety of workshops. Some are therapeutic, such as the *art feelings*, while others are simply for fun or to pursue hobbies, such as *collage* or *origami*. Every so often, special retreats are held to focus on special issues or provide residents with experiences of spiritual renewal.

Most TCs also provide in house schooling, some formal and others informal, to help residents increase their reading and writing competency. Some programs are able to confer a high school equivalency diploma or at least prepare members take the general equivalency diploma (GED) test. Most TCs for adolescents in the U.S. provide formal schooling for residents who are in long-term treatment.

Principle 6 – *The community provides interventions and activities that increase personal competency and survival skills*

The TC has simple steps for teaching work skills to residents when they first arrive in the community: (1) *show them exactly how assigned tasks are done,* (2) *let them do it,* (3) *give them corrective feedback,* and (4) *supervise them.* This is the standard model for teaching both simple and complex tasks. The rigidity of the procedure has an additional purpose of allowing residents to practice humility and "learn to follow instructions exactly as told." This is effective in promoting self-discipline, encouraging *pride in quality* of daily tasks, establishing consistency and timeliness in job functions, and learning how to work with others effectively. These are the rudimentary steps to learning and internalizing the value of work and work ethic.

The TC emphasizes teaching residents to develop the right attitude towards work and acquire good work ethic before teaching vocational skills. Residents often have to work to earn the privilege of working on special projects or signing up for vocational training. Developing a positive attitude and greater motivation enhances their ability to learn new skills, master any task, and perform better.

Even before cognitive-behavioral approaches became popular, the TC had already been using similar principles in training residents to acquire new behaviors and attitudes, social and coping skills, new work skills, and increased personal competency. The problem-solving strategies and social coping skills that residents learn in the TC help them avoid drug relapse and learn effective interpersonal as well as job-seeking skills.

Principle 7 – *The community provides interventions and activities that promote pro-social values and social reintegration*

Before residents reach the re-entry phase of treatment, they gradually assume increasing roles in helping to manage the daily operations of the community. By now they are trusted members of the upper echelon of the social hierarchy, working closely with staff, serving as role-models, and part of the "rational authority" of the TC. Their new found values are put to the test through the shift in their roles and increased levels of responsibility. Relapse and regressive behaviors can easily occur at this stage when residents have gained more freedom to move in and out of the community. In addition to the external sources of stress that residents are exposed to at this juncture of treatment, internal sources such as fear of failure, self-defeating tendencies, and other unresolved psychological issues can also contribute to stress. This stage is a prelude to the next crucial and even more challenging phase of treatment, reentry.

In the reentry phase, residents spend the greater part of their time seeking or holding a job or pursuing educational goals. While help is always within reach if needed, they are expected to use the skills they have learned from previous phases of treatment to cope with the demands of life outside the community. This is the final test of how much residents have learned from treatment and can serve as a gauge of how much more they need to learn to embark on their journey of lasting recovery.

Skilled counselors should be able to provide the right balance between using the limited structure of reentry and giving the residents the freedom to make informed choices. Counselors must help residents develop their own "structure" and rely on the pro-social values that they have hopefully internalized by this point of treatment. The value of the reentry and aftercare phases cannot be over emphasized. Not only is length of stay in treatment a consistent predictor of recovery status, but subsequent aftercare that follows reentry also improves the likelihood of positive treatment outcomes (Vanderplasschen, et al., 2013).

The road to complete recovery, if there is such a thing, is full of setbacks and is rarely a straight one. Slips and relapses in one form or another, and of various intensities, can be expected. When handled appropriately by counselors and residents, these can be good learning experiences that help solidify the residents' efforts towards lasting recovery.

Principle 8 – *The TC includes a family program that engages and provides support for families and significant others*

Addiction is not a disorder that affects only one person but rather one that also involves family members and significant others. When treating an addicted resident who has hopes of returning home after treatment, the TC must consider the risk that the family system might have contributed to or helped sustain the resident's addiction. On the other hand, when the family dynamics are not so pathological, ignoring an important source of support by failing to engage the family during treatment is a missed opportunity. Studies have repeatedly shown that those who can rely on a network of supportive social support are more likely to succeed in treatment and experience sustained recovery.

Even before research proved this practice to be sound, TCs had already involved families at some point in treatment. This is especially important among adolescents who are more likely to return home after treatment than adult residents. In cases where a parent, family member, or a significant other is also involved in substance abuse, efforts are made to offer them help. Residents are advised not to return home or maintain the relationship when a family member or significant other is actively abusing substances and is unwilling to get "clean." Association or a relationship with a substance abusing family member, significant other, or friend is a common reason for relapse by both adolescent and adult residents.

Whether or not there are substance abusing people in the residents' lives, it is important to educate the residents' family and friends about addiction and the TC treatment model. This is a good step in creating a treatment alliance between the TC and the family while treating residents. Most modern TCs have a family program as an adjunct to the TC program. Very often the program provides the needed educational and emotional support to families while one of their members is in treatment.

E. Treatment Outcome and Feedback

This component pertains to obtaining feedback through research to determine how the TC is working and whether it has been successful in accomplishing its goals. This component includes the following practice principle:

Principle 1 – *There is a system for monitoring and evaluating the effectiveness of the therapeutic community and its treatment outcomes*

The TC must monitor and determine how well it is able to meet its operational objectives and achieve its goal of providing effective treatment. In the last few decades, outcome research has helped to determine which factors contribute to positive outcomes. Foremost is treatment *retention.* There is a positive correlation between the amount of time residents spend in treatment and improvement in measures of *substance abuse, criminality, productive pursuits,* including measures of *psychopathology.* Although most of these studies were conducted in the U.S., the results may be generalized to other countries to a certain extent.

Keeping residents in treatment long enough for the TC processes to take effect is of great importance in determining treatment outcome. Monitoring dropout rates at significant points in treatment (e.g. thirty, sixty, or ninety days) can inform TCs as to when, where, what and how interventions can be employed to rectify this issue. Conducting regular resident satisfaction surveys can also provide a wealth of information on this matter.

A type of research that the TC can embark upon is an evaluation of how successful it is able to achieve its operational goals and objectives. This involves the TC social infrastructure – the treatment structure. The operational goals and objectives are directed towards creating the therapeutic environment necessary for the effective applications of the TC therapeutic tools and interventions. These goals and objectives are contingent upon forming the appropriate treatment context through factors such as the operations of the social hierarchy, the creation of community norms and their applications, the division and supervision of work, the effectiveness of the system of responsibility and accountability, and the general sustenance of the overall operations of the TC.

The results of outcome studies can provide good feedback regarding overall effectiveness and efficiency of a TC. They provide indicators for assessing whether resources have been well spent and in what areas outcomes can be improved upon.

Chapter 4

Community-as-Method
How the TC Social Hierarchy Works

The key concept of "community as treatment method" as it applies to the therapeutic community was first discussed by Rapoport (1960), who used the phrase "community as doctor" in his book under the same title, when he described the democratic TC treatment principles and approaches of the Maxwell Jones Model. In a similar vein, De Leon (2000) coined the phrase "community as method" in his classic book, *The Therapeutic Community: Theory, Model, and Method*, as it applies to the concept-based TC. The concept simply means *the use of the community as the primary "method" for bringing about change in the whole person.* The structure and processes necessary to accomplish this is described in the following discussion.

****

The social structure or hierarchy of the TC is the key element for implementing a "peer-driven" treatment process in a TC. For this reason, the TC for addictions is sometimes referred to as a *hierarchical TC.* The concept of "community-as-method" is operationalized by how TC staff are able to operate effectively at the three levels of staff operation

(See Chapter 3) and how the social structure is organized and functions as the backbone of the community. The TC's hierarchical organization facilitates the daily operations of the TC while creating the context for implementing the TC tools.

Aside from facilitating the operational functions of the TC, the social structure is also the most important means of empowering residents. The structure is a tool for helping residents achieve emotional and social maturity as the TC becomes the microcosm of society at large. An inherent assumption in this model is resident "self-efficacy." The TC views its residents as capable individuals with varying levels of motivation and dysfunction, but never as helpless or worthless individuals. The hierarchical system gives every resident a chance not only according to their talent but also based on their efforts and desire to prove themselves "deserving" of trust and responsibility in the running of the community.

Since the integrity of the TC as a treatment model hinges on the proper operations of the social structure, failure to form and sustain it often creates problems for the community. Like any human organization, the TC has its flaws. The social structure is vulnerable to the vagaries of human nature and can become corrupted. Setbacks in the TC, however, are viewed as potential learning experiences for both the individual and the community.

Four Overlapping Operational Functions

There are four overlapping operational functions that must interact to facilitate community-as-method and sustain its proper functioning: (1) *replication of the TC structure within work departments*, (2) *supervision of the social hierarchy*, (3) *the functions of the resident coordinator on duty (COD)*, and (4) *the functions of the staff-on-duty (SOD)*. Figure 4.1 provides a visual aid for understanding how the TC is organized and operates.

Figure 4.1 Components of the TC Hierarchical Social Structure

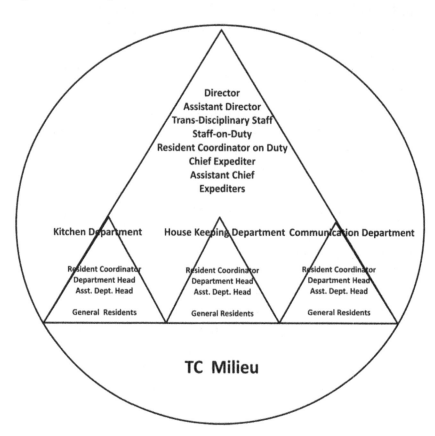

Replication of the TC Structure within Work Departments

Work departments are created to meet the various operational needs of a TC. The social organization of work departments, such as the kitchen department, communications, housekeeping, maintenance, etc., is a replica of the larger TC structure as depicted in Figure 4.1. The work departments replicate the structure and chain of command of the TC social hierarchy with its own internal chain of command as shown in Figure 4.2.

Figure 4.2 Work Department Hierarchical Structure

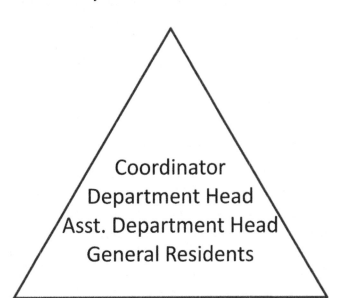

Coordinator
Department Head
Asst. Department Head
General Residents

The nature of work or job functions in the TC serves both operational and clinical goals. To achieve these goals the general functions or job description of the work departments must include both operational and clinical elements. Outlined below are the general functions of the work departments:

- To oversee resident performance in their job functions and program participation
- To monitor resident whereabouts
- To evaluate resident readiness to move up in the social structure
- To hold residents accountable for participation in program activities (e.g., Morning Meeting, Seminars, Encounter Group, Wrap-up, etc.) and clinical activities which are indicated in their treatment plan (e.g., Group Therapy, Counseling, etc.)
- To determine if residents deserve to be granted their requests for passes and privileges. (The criteria for moving up the social structure or earning privileges and passes are based on performance of job functions as well as engagement in treatment and participation

in various TC activities. The department head makes recommendations to the coordinator of the department for approval or denial of requests. The coordinator of the department makes the final recommendation to staff for passes and privileges.)

- To make recommendations for job changes (promotions or demotions)
- To hold residents accountable for any serious breaches of the house rules
- To develop and submit proposed work projects for staff approval

How effectively work departments are able to replicate the system of accountability of the larger TC social hierarchy determines how smoothly a TC will function. The coordinator and the department head of each department may organize special groups to resolve interpersonal issues among members or conduct interventions to provide support or hold members accountable for not living up to behavioral expectations. The high-ranking members of a department are accountable to staff and the community for serious breaches of house rules by residents within the department.

In this model, the position of "department head" is critical. This position directly supervises and provides guidance to the residents assigned to the department. These residents comprise the work crews who must be trained for their jobs, supervised, and monitored in their participation in treatment activities. Department heads are responsible to ensuring that residents are balancing the demands of their work and as well as their treatment needs. For example, residents who do their jobs well but avoid getting involved in Morning Meetings, fail to utilize the Encounter Group, or miss their clinical groups will have to be counseled or held accountable for not actively participating in their treatment. Residents must not only perform their job functions and comply with house rules, they must satisfy all of their clinical requirements and participate in the therapeutic activities spelled out in their treatment plans. Otherwise, they are not considered to be making progress and not "deserving" for rewards and privileges, for failing to meet program expectations. It is the job of the department head to utilize all available resources to help his crew members meet all of these expectations. In this role, he is supported by his assistant department head and supervised by the coordinator of the department. The position of department head is training for future coordinators.

Supervision of the TC Social Hierarchy

Staff supervision of the residents' social hierarchy is essential in maintaining its integrity and the community as a whole. It is through supervision that staff is able to provide the necessary training and guidance for the residents' leadership. It also serves as a deterrence of the potential abuse of power and authority such as the manipulation of the system for personal gain. Staff supervision must hold senior residents accountable for their performance while providing emotional support for those struggling to live up to program expectations. Supervision is provided during the weekly meeting conducted by the senior staff to discuss and approve requests for privileges, job changes, promotions or demotions, and other community business. Staff members also meet with the residents in leadership positions in regularly scheduled group sessions to settle interpersonal issues or conflict amongst the leadership.

Supervision of the social hierarchy occurs during departmental meetings, daily supervision of the coordinator's office by the Staff-on-Duty (SOD), and during the weekly meetings and group sessions of resident leaders. The staff assigned to oversee or supervise a work department monitors the daily departmental meeting and the department's daily operations. Staff assigned as Staff-on-Duty (SOD) for the day supervises and works with the coordinator's office, particularly the Coordinator on Duty (COD). The Staff-on-Duty and the Coordinator-on-Duty, in conjunction with the Chief Expediter, who is in-charge of implementing the daily schedule, manage the day-to-day business of running the community.

Functions of the Coordinator-on-Duty (COD)

It is important to understand that the upper echelon of the community, which is comprised of department coordinators, the chief and assistant chief expediters, department and assistant department heads, and expediters, is an extension of the staff or management. The staff team, who leads from behind, depends on the senior resident hierarchy that makes up this upper echelon to drive this peer-driven program.

The coordinators of the departments take turns in assuming the duties of the Coordinator-on-Duty (COD) while the Chief Expediter, his assistant, and a team of additional expediters see to the timely implementation of the daily schedule and rule compliance by community residents. The team of expediters becomes the "eyes and ears" of the community, providing guidance and direction to assist residents in living up to the community norms and rules. Serious behavioral issues are reported to the coordinator's office, investigated, documented, and then brought to the attention of the Staff-on-Duty (SOD) for final action.

It is the COD that coordinates the various activities of the work departments and receives all communications regarding important events and incidents that take place in the community. Important communications are relayed by the expediters to the Chief Expediter who determines which incidents require immediate action and filters these to the COD for processing and action.

The following are the functions or duties of the Coordinator-on-Duty (COD):

- To manage the Coordinator's Office
- To work with the Chief Expediter in the implementation of the daily schedule
- To work with the Chief Expediter in managing residents' behavioral issues "on the floor," (e.g., acting out, non-compliant behaviors, unsafe behaviors, etc.)
- To supervise the screening and documentation of incidents
- To conduct investigations or inquiries to verify incidents
- To supervise the Encounter Group Box and review all encounter slips with staff
- To work with and communicate important incidents to the SOD
- To organize confrontation groups when needed
- To supervise the recording of incidents in the Incident Book and Individual Incident Folders

- To implement all approved behavioral interventions
- To implement Initial Intake Interviews
- To coordinate searches and inventories of new residents' personal belongings with the SOD
- To supervise the upkeep of the Individual Incident Folders, Incident Books, Initial Intake Interview Forms and other documentations
- To coordinate house and fire runs, GIs, room searches, and other procedures designed to keep the community safe.

The Communications or Business Office Department provides assistance to the COD regarding clerical and administrative functions. The COD works with the Chief Expediter and his team with regards to organizing and scheduling confrontation groups, initial interviews, encounter groups, behavioral incidents, community surveillance, peer interventions, and other community activities.

Functions of the Staff-on-Duty (SOD)

The fourth and final operational function that supports the TC social structure involves the duties and functions of the Staff-on-Duty (SOD). TC staff members take turns in assuming this important daily function which oversees the implementation of the daily schedule and provides close supervision to the Coordinator's Office by working very closely with the COD and the Chief Expediter.

The SOD does not work directly with residents of the community. Instead, the social structure is allowed to perform its function by intervening or making recommendations for appropriate interventions when necessary. The SOD reviews and approves all behavioral interventions, sanctions, or learning experiences that the COD recommends for implementation. Senior residents, including the COD, do not have the authority to implement behavioral interventions on individuals or the community without staff approval.

The SOD is responsible for the key operational and clinical functions described below:

Operational Functions

- To supervise the COD and the implementation of the daily schedule
- To supervise the morning meeting, seminars, and other community activities
- To supervise, work with, and receive communications from the COD or the upper levels of the social structure regarding important incidents (e.g., serious behavioral or disciplinary issues, safety issues affecting the community, etc.)
- To monitor the upper levels of the social structure perform their job functions
- To receive feedback and recommendations from the COD regarding behavioral issues
- To receive feedback and recommendations from COD or upper levels of the social structure regarding implementation of behavioral interventions, encounter groups, formal confrontations, etc.
- To review and approve all behavioral interventions and sanctions

Clinical Functions

- To facilitate important TC group processes, e.g., encounter groups, behavioral interventions, initial interviews, formal inquiries or confrontations, etc.
- To confer with the COD or upper levels of the social structure regarding learning experiences, promotions, demotions, etc.
- To welcome new residents and facilitate initial interviews as well as discharge or exit interviews (for those leaving the TC)
- To recommend interventions regarding serious community issues to the Program Director or Deputy Director of the TC
- To take action on all incidents documented in the Incident Book that occur during the work shift
- To report important issues that occur during the shift to the staff team during the shift meeting
- To conduct individual interventions (e.g., crisis intervention, counseling, problem solving, referrals, etc.)

****

The Role and Functions of the TC Director

In addition to possessing management skills in operating a drug treatment program, it is highly preferable that the Director and his assistant are also knowledgeable on how the TC works. In operating a TC, it is difficult to compartmentalize treatment philosophy and organizational culture. This is a significant issue considering that the director has the final say in business and clinical matters that often have ramifications on the whole organization. The role of the director is not only to manage the treatment facility but also act as the figure head of the community who may have to address individual residents or the community regarding business or clinical matters pertaining to the operations of the TC. Familiarity with the TC concepts and practices promotes rapport and inspires confidence to both staff and residents. To illustrate this, please refer to the example below:

James is a director of *Viva TC.* He is a professional social worker who has limited knowledge of the TC. One of his counselors finds a bag of heroin and a hypodermic syringe hidden under a toilet sink in one of the rooms. There are five residents who sleep in the room. The counselor recommends the occupants of the room be immediately isolated and individually confronted by a panel of peers to get to the bottom of the matter. Urine samples may be obtained for drug testing if necessary. The director disagrees and decides instead that individual counseling may be a better approach to find the truth and to settle the matter. Additionally, he wants to call for a staff conference to get more feedback from other staff before taking any further action. The counselor protests and argues that doing so will only give the culprit/s time to discover that staff have found the stash, thus giving the errant resident/s enough time to develop a plan to mitigate or cover up their culpability. However, the director's decision prevails and his plan is implemented.

****

In above scenario the counselor's over-riding concern is the immediate containment of a very unsafe situation by utilizing a peer-driven process to address the issue. The director's approach reveals his limited knowledge and understanding of how the TC operates, especially under this type of situation.

Integrating Evidence-Based Practices into the TC
Putting the Horse Before the Cart

What is Evidence-Based Practice?

This catchphrase, as it applies to treatment, simply means that in order for a treatment model or intervention to be considered legitimate, it must pass the test of science. Many of the current and fashionable treatment tools and interventions of addiction, such as the *Addiction Severity Index, Motivational Interviewing, Motivational Enhancement Therapy, Relapse Prevention, Anger Management, Contingency Management Therapy, and Seeking Safety for PTSD and Substance Abuse,* as well as several other cognitive-behavioral therapies and assessment tools, have been found to be effective using experimental design studies. In the current climate surrounding treatment, programs that do not use evidence-based practices will have difficulty getting funding or even becoming recognized as legitimate treatment providers.

The Pitfalls

Drive-Thru Therapy

Basing therapeutic practices on science is one thing, but making them work for addicted individuals is another. The overriding concern for TC is how effectively evidence-based practices are integrated into the TC system in ways that do not undermine fidelity to the TC practice. Evidence-based interventions or therapies are not substitutes for the TC treatment processes but are complementary clinical tools that should enhance the treatment experience of residents. Knowledge of the bi-modal nature of the TC model, which is comprised of a therapeutic system on one hand and a set of therapeutic tools or methodologies on the other, is essential for a harmonious integration of evidence-based therapies into the TC arsenal of clinical tools. Please refer to Chapter 7 for a more in depth discussion of the bi-modal nature of the TC model.

Whether in an individual or group format, counselor skills and resident readiness remain two major factors for the positive outcome of therapeutic encounters. In addition, it is important not to lose the soul of therapy in the process of implementing evidence-based interventions. For counselor, it can be easy to lose touch of the nuances of each resident as they zip through the prescribed treatment curriculum. Drive-thrus have their time and place, but therapy is neither. It is unwise and unproductive to rush through the treatment process in the interest of time or money as rushing rarely saves either. Skilled counselors engage residents in ways that build rapport and increase their readiness for treatment.

Counselors must strive to create an ideal therapeutic environment where residents feel safe and assured that their needs will be heard and met. To achieve this, counselors must know when to put down the manual and be in the moment with a resident, when empathy can better serve the resident than sticking to the curriculum. A good counselor will be able to balance effective delivery of the didactic elements of the curriculum with good interpersonal skills. In using evidence-based interventions, it is important to be wary of turning therapy into an impersonal process and forgetting the basics of a good client-counselor relationship.

Another important issue for consideration is resident readiness to benefit from the treatment curriculum. Substance abusers also often suffer from cognitive deficits of either long or short-term duration, which may not be evident to inexperienced counselors. These deficits can impair the ability of these individuals to process information and benefit from treatment interventions. Some of these symptoms disappear after a period of sobriety while others may linger indefinitely. These factors need to be taken into consideration when determining the readiness of residents to begin treatment in some of the more involved and cognitively demanding evidence-based treatment practices.

The Context

The setting in which treatment occurs has a significant impact on how interventions are implemented. In an outpatient modality, counselors have little control or feedback regarding what happens once clients leave their offices other than what the clients are willing to share. Instances of substance use, how and with whom free time is spent, participation in unsafe activities, etc., are pertinent information in terms of program compliance and treatment progress. These are useful information that can be processed during counseling or group process. In an outpatient setting, counselors must rely on the client's honesty and willingness to self-disclose. Creating a treatment context that supports and facilitates honest self-disclosure is important. It is an important task for counselors to create the necessary therapeutic environment that facilitates the process of change in order for clients to benefit from interventions.

Similar requirements apply to residential settings. Residents in programs such as the TC must be grounded on the program structure and able to comply with the behavioral or normative requirements to benefit from any form of group process. TC residents who have not adjusted to the program structure or achieved the required level of acculturation can be very disruptive in counseling or groups. TC residents must complete the program orientation process and demonstrate adequate levels of behavioral and emotional stability before being assigned to specialized or evidence-based groups.

Who are the Consumers?

Understanding the different types of residents found in a TC and what they bring to treatment will help gauge resident needs and determine suitable interventions. Appropriate screening, assessment, and treatment planning should be able to help in making this determination. The majority of individuals who are treated in a TC suffer from substance abuse, and a significant number come from the criminal justice system. Their psychosocial and clinical backgrounds are significant factors that contribute to their treatment outcomes. The counselors and group facilitators should be sufficiently knowledgeable about the residents' backgrounds before residents are assigned to start treatment in evidence-based counseling or groups.

The following are common characteristics of TC residents that require consideration:

- Severity of their substance abuse and its effects on their behavior, emotions, and way of thinking
- Readiness for treatment and motivation for change, which includes levels of engagement in treatment and knowledge of the recovery process
- Prior treatment experience, which includes history of prior recovery or failure in treatment
- Mental health and psychological status, e.g., presence of co-occurring disorders, medications, and level of cognitive functioning
- Legal status and criminal propensities, e.g., legal issues, history of incarcerations, etc.
- Habilitation versus rehabilitation needs

The Curriculum

Counselors should make an assessment of the treatment curriculum to determine how it fits into the TC model, whether it will meet resident needs, and the requirements for its implementation. The following are simple guidelines for reviewing evidence-based curricula:

Level of sophistication - Are the concepts discussed in the curriculum easy to grasp? Do they readily relate to the goal of recovery and the resident's progress towards recovery? The levels of curricula can be categorized into *basic, intermediate,* or *advanced* to help determine which and when residents are ready for each curriculum.

Ease of use – Is the curriculum easy to follow, read, and implement? Is the counselor's guide user-friendly or the resident workbook within the reading and comprehension level of the resident? How are the sessions or group sessions designed? Are they stand-alone or sequential, where each session builds on previous sessions? What is the minimum number of sessions required to expect a positive outcome? Does the curriculum format lend itself to either individual or group sessions?

Relevance - How does the curriculum contribute to building the foundation for long-term recovery? How does it relate to the TC processes and reinforce the recovery process?

Training requirements for facilitators - What is the required educational or professional training for the facilitators? How much time is involved in training facilitators? What are the requirements for on-going supervision?

Preparation

To enhance positive outcomes, it is important that residents are poised to benefit from treatment interventions. Relevant information that pertains to pre-requisites may include behavioral or psychological readiness of the resident, such as completion of a treatment phase and level of treatment compliance. The intervention must be indicated in the treatment plan.

Implementation

To avoid a disjointed implementation of evidence-based groups and interventions within the TC programming, they must be considered parallel processes. The TC staff and counselor must be familiar with the TC protocol and the protocol of specific evidence-based interventions before facilitating them. For example, a resident who admits to using substances during a home pass in a *Relapse Prevention Group* should be allowed to process the event and finish the group. Staff should not stop the process and remove the resident from the group for confrontation for violating the TC rules. The TC protocol for handling this violation takes over only after the group, when the resident is held accountable for violating the community norms. Knowing which protocol takes precedence over the other in a given situation is important.

Staff should also be familiar with each resident's progress in the TC and use this information to guide which skills they teach during the group sessions. For example, a resident who has been cited for repeatedly violating TC house rules might benefit from a *Relapse Prevention Group* or *Trauma Group* by learning coping skills that might help him adapt better. Likewise, a resident who finds it difficult to avoid lashing out at his peers during his job might benefit from an *Anger Management Group.* In both situations, the residents will benefit from working with a counselor and peers in the group to determine how various learning experiences imposed on them have failed and which individual approaches or community interventions might help them. Evidence-based groups will mean little unless staff is able to relate the material to real experiences within the TC and show how they are interconnected.

In order to help residents make connections between their behaviors in the TC milieu, the skills being taught, and the skills' relevance to their eventual return to society, staff must have knowledge of both the TC processes and evidence-based practices. For staff to achieve such a level of expertise, they must remain actively engaged in TC operations, become familiar with how residents respond to the TC process, and be able to use evidence-based technology in a consistent and congruent fashion.

Outcome Evaluation

It is good practice to determine treatment outcome. This can be accomplished in different levels. Counselors should document outcomes related to the goals of a particular therapy or intervention. For example, how has teaching the development of skills in anger management helped to reduce "acting-out behaviors" within the community among those residents who completed the treatment course? Monitoring the level and frequency of behavioral incidents in the community in the "*incident logbook*" can be a good way to gather this information.

Counselors may also perform outcome evaluations based on improvements in treatment compliance and chronicle treatment progress based on a set of criteria, e.g., program participation, behavioral incidents, job performance, negative toxicology, etc.

Finally, outcomes related to treatment retention and completion should also be documented. This will help strengthen the evidence-based knowledge around which practices contribute to resident retention and treatment completion rates.

Enhancements

Outcome evaluation will also aid in determining in which areas TCs need to "tweak" their practice or implementation of interventions to increase success. This will help to identify what adjustments are needed in the implementation of a TC to harmonize the evidence-based treatment curriculum with the TC program process. In order to do this, practitioners should be thoroughly familiar with the intervention model as well as the treatment context of the TC. Knowledge of both models is necessary to ensure fidelity to practice.

There should also be a plan for program sustainability. On-going training and education through *booster training* can enhance practitioner skills under the supervision of qualified clinicians.

Modern Challenges of the Therapeutic Community

The following list of challenges is by no means exhaustive. These are challenges that have been encountered in U.S.-based TCs as well as some, but not all, foreign TCs. The differences in the kind and extent of challenges encountered by various TCs across the globe are determined by socio-economic and political factors, such as government drug control policies, support for public drug programs, societal causal attributions of and attitudes towards drug abuse problems, addiction, and the treatment of addicted-individuals, etc.

Misunderstanding of the TC Principles

TC practitioners often differ in their understanding of the TC principles. The common route for educating about the TC philosophy and practice is experiential, either from personal treatment experience or from working in a TC, or both. This highly subjective process, which is influenced by personal philosophy, has resulted in inconsistencies in processing TC information and practicing its treatment principles. Even among professionals who work in therapeutic communities, few are motivated to delve into available literature on the subject. Early TC leaders discouraged the questioning of the TC principles and practices;

instead, they emphasized "blind faith" in the program and its leadership. In doing so, they initiated a weak scholarly tradition among frontline staff to examine the basis of the TC philosophy and practices. This has not only stalled the development of the TC but can also contribute to weak foundations that are easier to corrupt.

Another reason for the limited understanding of the TC is the fact that most studies on the TC are conducted by scholars who rarely practice the trade. This, coupled with the fact that few practitioners self-educate, has resulted in very little trickle down of evidence-based knowledge to practitioners. The experiential perspective that can only be gleaned from personal practice is often missing in these studies. The inadequate transmission of TC knowledge and the paucity of literature on the subject have contributed to the problem of bad practice and the misuse of many TC interventions. For example, to shape problematic behaviors of residents, the TC philosophy calls for a non-punitive approach called the "learning experience." However, the implementation of the learning experience in many TCs has become punitive and sometimes even abusive. It loses its learning quality and efficacy when proper practice protocols are not observed. A TC tool will erode its efficacy without proper implementation or when it is left in the hands of untrained practitioners, whose ignorance of the TC can cause them to inadvertently adulterate its practice.

Modification of the TC to comply with regulations

Complaints regarding bad practices have led to the revisions of some TC procedures with no regard to fidelity, and the restrictions imposed on some TC practices have exacerbated the issue. Due to bad practices, some behavior-shaping strategies have been forbidden due to their misuse. However, when applied correctly, some of these strategies were effective means of curtailing disruptive behaviors, especially in residents who were historically difficult to manage. Deprived of effective means of social control, the TC has become weak and ineffective in managing difficult or unmotivated residents.

There is also often poor communication within TC organizations resulting in conflicting or inconsistent policies. Directives given by management to frontline clinical staff can be vague regarding how new regulations should be interpreted. Not only do they often fail to provide guidance on how the TC should adapt its practice to comply with regulations that have been imposed on their program, they also rarely provide coherent guidelines for alternative practices or how to compensate for modifications in the TC practice.

Failure to keep up with new knowledge and practices

TC practitioners have failed to keep up with the growing knowledge and practices in the field of addiction treatment and incorporate them into their practice to enhance TC interventions. The lack of knowledge on how the TC processes work has resulted in disjointed applications of even evidence-based practices within the TC. To remain true to both the TC principles and evidence-based practices requires a full understanding of how the TC works and how evidence-based practices may be blended into traditional practices to enhance the TC's treatment approach. Doing so can strengthen a TC by contributing to the development of a more comprehensive treatment approach.

For example, *Motivational Interviewing* techniques can be incorporated into the Emotional or Initial Interview or into Peer Interventions to mitigate the intrusive nature of the two treatment tools. Also, *Motivational Incentives* or *Contingency Management Therapy* can complement the TC's *System of Privileges* by providing sources of motivation during the early phases of treatment while new residents are working to earn the more structured privileges of the TC. Well-adapted practitioners will also understand that a trauma-informed TC process is necessary given the prevalence of trauma-related disorders, such as PTSD, among substance-abuse treatment populations. The TC can be strengthened by not only staying current with the growing knowledge of addiction treatment but also using that knowledge to inform the TC treatment approach.

The emphasis on "safety" during the implementation and practice of TC interventions must also guide practice. For example, the practice of "*debriefing*" the community when serious house rules are broken, such as use of substances or acts of violence, must be standard practice. Clear behavioral boundaries must be established to preserve the safety of the community, such as terminating residents from treatment for serious violations of cardinal rules or endangering personal safety or the community.

The absence of professional certification specific to TC practitioners

The standard training for professional certification in addiction is not sufficient to produce adequately trained TC staff. To acquire proficiency in the practice of the TC, candidates should complete a comprehensive curriculum that includes theory and practice. The training design must balance academic or classroom learning with supervised experiential training. To become certified, the candidates should complete a two-year supervised internship or work in a TC to develop sufficient proficiency as a TC practitioner. Regular supervision of TC staff by an experienced TC practitioner must be standard practice in all TC. Staff members should also have an individualized training development plan that is reviewed yearly as part of an annual performance evaluation.

Some TC practices are not compatible with the practices of some professions

Many professionals currently working in TCs are hired primarily to comply with funding requirements. As a result, the staffing patterns of many of the TCs have changed, with traditionally trained medical and mental health staff dominating the field, while the number of paraprofessional ex-addict staff is declining. These professionals are rarely required to be proficient in the practice of the TC, and since many are trained largely on the medical and mental health model, their professional culture often clashes with the TC's principles, particularly the practice of "community-as-method."

Staff roles and functions in the TC are different from traditional medical/mental health models. For example, staff self-disclosure in therapy is an accepted practice in the TC but is not favored by many traditionally trained professionals. To be emotionally invested in the resident's recovery and be a reliable supportive figure are vital components of working with TC residents. Many traditionally trained professionals are not comfortable with the TC's informal and "close" collaboration between staff and residents while implementing the TC processes. The TC's emphasis of minimizing the "we-they" dichotomy between staff and residents and its dismantling of protocols that keep staff segregated from residents within the TC milieu can be anxiety-provoking for some professionals.

Professionals who bring with them different world-views and disciplines must be unified under the TC philosophy and core values. The lack of organized training and orientation of new staff in some TCs and the inability of management to induce them to learn and become proficient in TC has posed the greatest challenge in implementing and practicing the TC with fidelity.

The TCs' development into a business model

The shift towards a business model that has come with hiring management staff who are trained in business but lack clinical knowledge and experience to manage the TC has not contributed to its viability and survival. Under the current economic climate, where fiscal health of the organization is a primary concern, the business aspect of the TC often takes precedence over its clinical integrity. Filling beds and maximizing billable services have become priorities and have helped drug programs to survive financially, often at the expense of sound clinical practice. These business strategies are prevalent even though these practices can be highly disruptive and weaken the TC treatment process. Often, the business solution is a short-term fix but with long-term negative consequences to the overall health of the organization. The inability of the TC management to strike a balance between business concerns and treatment integrity is perhaps the greatest challenge that the TC faces today.

The moral and ethical dilemmas that arise from using a purely business model is rarely discussed. When a drug treatment program struggles to survive and business plans are put together, there is seldom any serious effort put towards analyzing how contingency plans might negatively impact vital services for residents who are already vulnerable, or add to the burden of an already beleaguered treatment staff. There are currently few mechanisms within the TC organization to temper a purely business driven model and keep treatment true to its mission of "saving lives." While practitioner behavior and professional practice are subject to scrutiny and must adhere to the "ethics of the profession," the ethical or moral principles against which management or executives of treatment organizations are held accountable are lacking. When poorly devised policies are implemented, with clinically disastrous consequences, management is rarely held effectively accountable.

An increasing number of clients with co-occurring disorders

Finding the right fit between resident needs and treatment model requires a thorough screening and assessment process in which prospective residents' treatment needs as well as their abilities to benefit from a particular treatment model are assessed. Because of the significant increase in the number of substance abuse clients with co-occurring mental disorders and/or criminogenic backgrounds, TCs must adapt to meet the needs of these populations. Proper screening and assessment must be implemented to determine the severity of these co-occurring disorders and the ability of a particular TC to treat them. Evidence-based intake protocols that include the use of reliable screening and assessment tools should guide admission decisions. Failing to observe this sound practice often results in the admission of residents who are not appropriate for treatment in a TC. This not only leads to difficulties in meeting their needs but can also result in the inability of the TC to manage and control residents in the treatment milieu.

High rates of staff turnover

Addiction counseling or therapy is a highly demanding field, and staff burnout is common due to heavy workload and the effects of vicarious traumatization. The profession demands a lot from its practitioners both academically and emotionally. In addition to a thorough knowledge of abused substances and their pharmacological effects, counselors must also understand the nature of addiction, addictive disorders, and various addiction therapies. These subjects alone cover a very broad field, but when you add the human dimension of the addicted individuals and the range of psychopathologies that are highly correlated with substance use and addiction, the field of knowledge that needs mastery becomes even broader. These qualifications, combined with the counseling skills that are necessary to work effectively with a highly unmotivated, often disenfranchised and character-disordered population, define a profession that requires expertise in multiple, overlapping disciplines. On top of all these factors, addiction counseling and therapy is not a lucrative profession, and practitioners are rarely adequately financially compensated for their work.

A large number of addiction professionals leave the field before retirement but after they have amassed considerable experience (White, 1993). When these professionals and paraprofessionals switch career paths, they take with them valuable experiences that could have otherwise enriched the field of addiction treatment and the therapeutic community.

Hybridization of the TC

As I discussed earlier, hybrid TCs that do not conform to sound TC practices often have incongruent elements (See Chapter 2). Hybridization can result to adaptive or disruptive elements of the TC model. The lack of consistency between the TC treatment principles and actual practice often undermines treatment effectiveness. Without fidelity to practice, it is also difficult to evaluate treatment outcome or program effectiveness, which further hinders the development of the practice.

While there is risk of the TC model becoming corrupted due to hybridization on one hand, on the other, it demonstrates its ability to adapt to the changing landscape of drug abuse problem and its treatment. The TC's flexible and adaptive character adds to its universal appeal. Provided the TC philosophy is understood and its practice principles adhered in theory and in practice, adaptations and innovations made to the TC model are less likely to result to a dysfunctional model. Furthermore, the intuitive elements of the TC model often guide those who truly understand its fundamental philosophy to remain faithful to its spirit and practice.

A better approach to designing TC outcome research

It is important for outcome studies to incorporate a different way of viewing the TC. The research design must take into account the two major overlapping and reciprocal aspects of the TC model as both a social system and a treatment approach. The efficacy of its social system, which provides the structure for implementing "community-as-method," is unrivaled, especially for treating addicted individuals who are averse to traditional structure, and research studies have documented the effectiveness of prison-based TCs. The structured treatment context provided by the social system of the TC is crucial in order for TC interventions and treatment tools to be effective. The quality of the social system is highly influenced and determined by the proper implementation of the TC treatment interventions (the application of the TC tools), and reciprocally, the effectiveness of the TC tools is determined by the quality of the social context. In other words, the TC tools won't work in the absence of a TC environment, and the therapeutic quality of the environment depends on the effective use the TC tools.

Shorter treatment duration and high dropout rates

The TC is a learning model that requires educating its residents so they become familiar with its system and acculturate to its treatment approach. The faster new residents learn the system, the more integrated they become into the community. Educating residents about the nature of their condition and the necessary interventions that will facilitate change is an integral part of the treatment process. All these processes require time, and residents learn at their own individual pace. Treatment motivation is a major factor in this learning process. The more motivated residents are, the faster they will engage in treatment and be able to participate in the daily TC routines. However, the typical TC resident often struggles with ambivalence between remaining in and leaving treatment during the first month or two. This is especially true for residents who have been referred to the TC by criminal justice agencies who often feel coerced to getting help as their only alternative to treatment is jail time. They usually choose treatment, but then often they pursue this goal half-heartedly, with no genuine desire to explore the real cause of their problems. These residents often do just enough to get by without any real efforts towards change. Due to the shorter treatment durations, the greater portion of treatment time goes towards motivating residents to invest energy into their treatment, but when adequate motivation is finally achieved their treatment time is often coming to a close. Many who never develop genuine motivation for change end up leaving early or getting discharged from treatment for program rule violations or other non-compliant behaviors.

Effective early resident engagement strategies and the efficient delivery of coherent drug treatment interventions are severely lacking in many TCs. High dropout and low completion rates are factors that negatively impact TC treatment outcomes.

Inability to sustain an uninterrupted treatment process

The first two months of residential treatment is a crucial period for integrating residents into the TC structure and treatment process. Their complete immersion into a dynamic and pervasive TC process is important in laying down a solid foundation for a recovery-oriented treatment. Uninterrupted exposure to the treatment milieu, free from distractions, is necessary for recovering residents whose motivation for change is often in a constant state of flux. This initial condition is crucial in helping to establish the path to recovery for residents who are still uncommitted and ambivalent about giving up their addictive behavior and ways of thinking. To accomplish this, a dynamic and pervasive TC treatment process must be available. However, creating this important condition in a TC that has little or no ability to curtail outside interferences and movements of residents in and out of the treatment environment is almost impossible. Treatment boundaries must be established and counter-productive outside influences that dilute the treatment process must be curtailed.

The challenges facing the TC are numerous and complex. Some of these are external forces which the TC has little or no control over. However, many are within the TC's ability to overcome given adequate determination and political will to act on what is necessary.

Chapter 7

Theory-Grounded Therapeutic Community

Part I

In the Beginning . . .

Attempts to ground the Therapeutic Community into a particular set of psychological theories have been an afterthought. Synanon, the recognized origin of the concept-based or hierarchical therapeutic community, was not launched based on a set of well thought-out psychological principles about human behavior and the process of change. The only explicit, recognizable conceptual framework was that of AA or Alcoholics Anonymous, thanks to Charles E. Dederich's affiliation to it as an alcoholic. Dederich led a band of alcoholics and heroin addicted individuals to conduct their own "meetings" with a semblance of an AA meeting. These meetings eventually evolved into something resembling more of a Dederich's group process imbued with his own highly confrontational style, and the rest is history.

There were no clear treatment principles to guide practice in Synanon. Nonetheless, some of the guiding notions and underlying principles of the Twelve-Step paradigm were faintly discernible. The most significant of which was the concept of "self-help." Dederich developed explanatory principles for what they did as they went along, borrowing ideas and language from American thinkers, such as Emerson, Thoreau, Maslow, Hayakawa, and concepts from eastern philosophy and psychological theories prevalent at the time. These included psychoanalysis, behaviorism, social learning, and psychodrama, among others. He was attracted to eastern thought particularly Zen Buddhism and was fascinated by the writings of Lao-tzu, especially the *Way of Life*. Synanon's intellectual base was eclectic. Perhaps, it was the lack of allegiance to a particular school of thought that allowed Synanon to innovate, and the reliance on unfettered clinical intuition that made the Synanon approach unique and effective.

There were homegrown theories (Perfas, 2004) prevalent in the early days of the TC which were primarily centered on the addicted person's faulty self-image, different ways of how individuals handle feelings, types of responses to stressful or threatening situations, psychological encapsulation, "acting-as-if," and verbal assaults directed to the addicted person's maladaptive behavior (and not the personality).

The TC as a Social System and a Therapeutic Model

Before proceeding to the task of grounding the TC to psychological theories that are consistent with its treatment philosophy and practices, it is important to recognize that the TC is both a *treatment system* or *social system* and a *treatment model* (Perfas, 2004). The failure to recognize these two major features of the TC has compounded the understanding of the TC and its general effectiveness. As a treatment system the TC provides the organizing principles on how and when therapy or treatment is implemented. The organizing principles create a context that is conducive for therapeutic processes to occur. In addition to its affinity to other self-help treatment models, it is unique in its use of the "community" as the primary source of healing. Social system perspective is helpful in understanding this paradigm (Norlin & Chess, 1997; Perfas, 2004).

As a treatment model, it consists of overlapping behavioral, psychological, social, and cognitive strategies or approaches designed to effect change in addictive behaviors. The social system consists of components, such as the social hierarchy or structure and physical plant within which treatment or its clinical approaches operate, and together they operationalize the concept of "community-as-method." As a treatment model, it is flexible and capable of accommodating interventions derived from a variety of sources, provided those interventions are "fully blended" within the TC system. The treatment system and the clinical approaches overlap and are reciprocal in such a way that the integrity of the system is determined by the proper implementation of the treatment tools and vice versa. To borrow from Yalom (1995), the two features of the TC together provide the "mechanisms and the conditions for change."

The TC as a treatment system and treatment approach has been successful in providing a credible treatment environment with effective social control strategies for the difficult to treat substance abuse population. The TC has been successfully used in prison and community-based drug treatment programs in many countries. However, outcome studies on the TC have focused on its effectiveness as a whole, very rarely on its therapeutic processes (Simpson, 2004). Disentangling the two overlapping, reciprocal elements for research purposes will not be easy but also not impossible. There is no doubt that sufficient time spent in treatment in credible TC programs has consistently produced positive outcomes in reducing substance use and criminal behavior, and also increased engagement in productive activities by substance abuse clients. Little is known regarding the exact aspects of the TC and how they have contributed to these positive outcomes. What we know for sure is that positive outcomes are associated with the length of time spent in treatment, otherwise known as *retention.* Conceptualizing the TC as *bi-modal*, consisting of system (structure) and treatment approaches or interventions (clinical) may help us examine these features separately or concurrently and determine how they contribute to effectiveness and outcome. This will refine our understanding of its operational and therapeutic processes and how they contribute to outcomes. We know from experience and observations that TC structure, or a functional system of accountability, is necessary to create and maintain a safe treatment environment where genuine therapy has a better chance of happening. The ability of practitioners to implement the TC treatment processes and evidence-based practices with fidelity is determined by the quality and stability of the treatment environment.

*****

Grounding the TC on Psychological Theories

Originally the TC was conceptualized as a social-psychological model for the treatment of addiction. It has its own set of assumptions or views on addiction, the addicted-person, the change or recovery process, and the treatment method (De Leon, 2000). It borrowed heavily from and was influenced by various social and psychological theories, although it has its own social-psychological native theories about therapy, the drug-addicted person, and the nature of addiction (Sugarman, 1974; Perfas, 2004). The influence of psychological theories that held sway during the TC's formative years, such as psychoanalysis, behavioral psychology, social learning, humanistic, gestalt, psychodrama, etc., can be discerned from some of the TC interventions and terminologies.

Humanistic Psychology

Humanistic psychology places emphasis on the characteristic that are unique to humans, rather than those that we share with other animals. It focuses on the totality and wholeness of the individual and not any singular distinct feature, such as cognitive development (Norlin & Chess, 1997). Humanistic elements were incorporated into the TC model and enriched the treatment approach, such as psychodrama, transactional analysis, new identity process, bonding therapy, bio-energetic group, etc. (Kooyman, 1993). In Italy, *Progetto Uomo (Project Man)*, contributed to the development of humanism with a Christian strain, a philosophy that puts the human being in the center of his own history, stressing the importance of mental, psychological, and spiritual growth. *Progetto Uomo* had far reaching influence on the TC movement in Italian and Spanish-speaking countries in Europe and Latin America (Soyez & Broekaert, 2005).

A prominent humanistic theorist was Abraham Maslow who developed his need theory based on his study of those who were self-actualized. He posits that man's human nature is good or at least neutral, and not bad or driven by animal aggression or sexual impulse (Maslow, 1970). His postulate of a *hierarchy of needs,* i.e., *survival, safety and security, social belonging, self-esteem, and self-actualization,* serves as a foundation of a hierarchy of values. These needs are arranged in an ascending survival priority beginning with the basic needs for physical survival, such as food, followed by safety and security, social belonging, self-esteem and culminating in the need for self-actualization or the realization of one's unique potentials, referred to as *meta* need which transcends the basic needs and is concerned with the individual's full potentials.

Maslow (1976) outlines the basic things people need to thrive in their social environment. First, is the need to feel safe and protected, feelings of safety and being cared for is foremost. Second is the need of belonging to a family, a clan, or a group that bestows a sense of belonging and acceptance or being part of a larger entity. Third is to experience the feeling of affection and to feel that they are worth loving. Lastly is the need to experience respect and esteem from other people. Maslow, in his visit to Daytop Village, observed that TC was effective because it offered an environment where it was possible to experience these feelings.

It is common observation among new residents in the TC that they are initially more preoccupied with sensual gratifications, such as eating, sleeping, resting, etc., while trying to fit in and adapt to the TC environment. After they have successfully integrated themselves into the community and feel secure with their place in it, they begin to seek social status (positions) within the TC social hierarchy by conforming to the social norms and community values. It fulfills the need for respect and esteem from others. Further down the line, when they begin to feel grounded in the recovery process and have experienced a period of sobriety, they focus their attention beyond just staying sober and drug-free. They become interested in more spiritual pursuits or the exploration of careers and interests that can possibly help them realize their potentials (Perfas, 2004).

Family Therapy

During the early phase of treatment, TC residents have no contact with their families and much of the outside world. This allowed them to devote their full attention to the task of adjusting to the TC environment and grappling with any residual ambivalence they might have about getting help. This time also allowed staff to get to know the residents' potential family or social support network that could be harnessed during treatment. In the early days of the TC, new residents' contact with their families was curtailed to minimize any negative influence they might have on the residents. This was particularly true for those who came from chaotic families whose dysfunctions might have contributed to the substance abuse of the resident. This stance changed when the TC realized that the family was often the only meaningful source of support and the place where residents would likely return after treatment, especially adolescents. Since gradual reentry was needed to prepare residents for reintegration with the outside world, and their families were often the only readily available resource to provide housing, the family could no longer be ignored. The importance of engaging the family and assessing their potential role in treatment became obvious.

Parents or families of residents began organizing themselves into Family Associations. Although closely affiliated with the TC organization, they often operated independently. These associations took charge of developing family programs, with explicit help from the TC. Family programs were organized as adjunct to the TC program designed to educate families about the TC, provide mutual support among families, and offer interventions to family members who may have substance abuse problems themselves. Substance abusing family members or significant others presented challenges when the residents were ready to have contact with them. Family interventions were conducted to address any immediate issues and to improve communications between the family and the resident, as well as assess any potential risks presented by substance abusing family members. The family program did not necessarily subscribe to any school of family therapy, and rather the family sessions were more in line with family counseling, focused on problem solving or reestablishing communications between residents and their families or significant others. These sessions were called "family encounters," which were facilitated by TC staff or consultant staff, and borrowed some elements from the *Encounter Group*.

Family therapy did not take hold in the adult program of many second generation TCs. Although its practice was not discouraged and sometimes even considered a vital intervention, the practice of family therapy was left to the discretion of those staff with the training and motivation to include it as part of their clinical repertoire.

Family therapy, on the other hand, was more likely to be incorporated into the adolescent TC program. Salvador Minuchin's *Structural Family Therapy* model and *Solution Focused Family Therapy* were popular in the Daytop adolescent program at one time. Solution Focused Family Therapy was favored for its shorter term timeframe and focus on individual and family strengths versus problems and difficulties. It served as a good counterpoint for the TC's tendency to focus on problems and shortcomings. Unlike some European TCs, particularly the Italian's, which incorporated elements of family therapy into the TC practice, family therapy did not have a similar widespread influence on the American TC.

Psychoanalytic Theory

Although the early TCs, particularly Synanon, relied heavily on community or group process to influence change, it used psychoanalytic terms and concepts to describe human behavior and motivation, i.e., id, ego, superego, the unconscious, etc. In group process, interpersonal behavioral responses and strategies were described in terms such as "defense mechanism," "regression," "rationalization," "projection," "identification," "projective identification," "transference," "counter-transference," etc. The TC did not always adhere to traditional psychoanalytic practice, but used concepts such as *projection, identification,* or *displacement* and encouraged community members to act these behaviors out verbally during a General Meeting or an Encounter Group to bring out hidden or provoked feelings from an anxiety-laden situation, such as someone using substances in the community or committing other unsafe behaviors. Psychoanalytic theory provided the language for understanding and explaining internal determinants of behavior. To explain and understand determinants of overt behavior, the TC turned to behavioral theory.

Behavior and Cognitive-Behavior Theory

Behavior therapy developed as a reaction to the Freudian psychoanalytic approach to psychotherapy sometime in the mid-20th century. The major criticism against psychoanalytic theory and practices was the lack of empirical evidence to support its theory and its effectiveness. The behaviorists held the view that what went on inside the person's mind was not directly observable or measurable for any meaningful empirical study. They looked for replicable connections between events or *stimuli* in the environment and observable and measurable *responses* from subjects being studied. The domain of learning theory, a prevalent psychological model at the time, was to establish general principles that explain how subjects (people or organisms) learn new associations between stimuli and responses. Using this model, behaviorists steered away from abstract concepts about how the mind works, i.e. unconscious processes, unconscious motivations, etc., and instead employed principles of learning theory to modify behavior and emotional reactions. For example, instead of using psychoanalysis to treat phobia or an anxiety disorder, the behaviorist employed such techniques as *systematic desensitization* for cure (Westbrook, et al., 2011).

The initial success of behavior therapy in treating anxiety disorders, because of its objective procedures, measurable outcomes, and cost-effectiveness, did not satisfy some who believed that mental processes such as thoughts, beliefs, interpretations, etc. are equally compelling facts of life that cannot be ignored. This dissatisfaction over the limitations of a purely behavioral approach to human behaviors and mental disorders led to what is known in the 1970s as the "cognitive revolution." What came out of that period was a new approach that we now know as *cognitive-behavior therapy* or CBT. It is a model that combined elements of behavior therapy and cognitive therapy while maintaining an empirical approach to psychology and therapy.

Basic Principles of Cognitive-Behavior Therapy (CBT)

The following are considered the most basic beliefs or principles on which CBT is founded (Westbrook, et al., 2011):

The Cognitive Principle

The belief that people's behaviors and emotional reactions are influenced by their thoughts, beliefs, and interpretations about themselves or their situations, in other words, the meaning they ascribe to the events in their lives. These are the *cognitive* elements of human experience. This is illustrated in Figure 7.1 (Westbrook et al., 2011):

Figure 7.1 Cognitive Principle

THE COGNITIVE MODEL

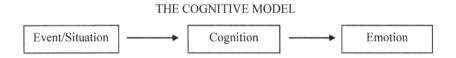

The Behavioral Principle

This principle is the legacy of behavior therapy, in which CBT maintains that behavior or action is important in changing or maintaining psychological states. Thus, behavior has a significant influence on one's emotions and thinking, such that altering one's action can be an effective means of changing thoughts and emotions. Principles 1 and 2, are illustrated in Figure 7.2.

Figure 7.2 Cognitive-Behavioral Principle

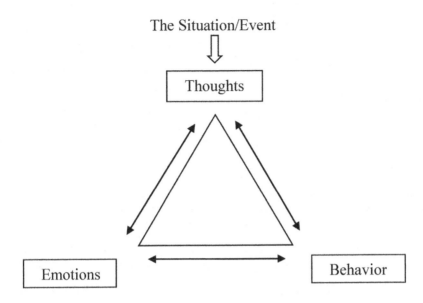

We can change how we feel about certain things by either altering our behavior or our thoughts. For example, if the sight of dogs elicits fear, you can learn to gradually approach dogs rather than avoid them. In due time, your fear will diminish as you learn that not all dogs bite. Or you can change your negative thoughts about dogs by challenging your fear and reminding yourself that you know of many instances where dogs are employed to help people, e.g., "seeing dogs," "bomb-sniffing dogs," etc., and friends who have and love dogs. If they are such vicious animals nobody would have them as pets.

The Continuum Principle

CBT believes that psychological dysfunctions can be viewed in a continuum with one end representing normal processes and the other representing its extreme. This view considers the more pathological states not as manifestations of an entirely separate category of pathology but rather a position in the continuum. This view minimizes stigmatization in a person with mental disorder and prevents viewing him less of a person.

The "Here and Now" Principle

CBT's focus of treatment is in what is currently happening (in the present) and what processes are maintaining the problem, instead of the processes that happened in the distant past that led to the development of the problem. The main target of treatment is the symptoms themselves and the processes that maintain them, and how those processes can be changed.

The Interacting Systems Principle

CBT views psychological problems as interactions between various systems within the individual and the environment. These systems are as follow: *cognition, affect* or *emotion, behavior,* and *physiology.* These systems interact with each other and include the physical or social environment, e.g., family, culture, economy, etc., in a complex feedback processes. Analyzing these interactions allows us to describe problems in a richer context to address specific aspects of the problem, and also allows us to determine when one or more systems are not interrelated with the others.

The Empirical Principle

CBT believes that theories and treatment practices should be amenable to scientific validation to be considered evidence-based, comply with ethical principles of sound practice, and provide economical and cost-effective services.

Levels of Cognition

One of the hallmarks of cognitive-behavior therapy is the elaboration of the cognitive concept into *levels of cognition.* Westbrook and colleagues (2011) provide the following classification:

Negative Automatic Thoughts

These are specific thoughts accessible to consciousness that arise spontaneously in various situations, which often have negative effects on our mood. They are negative imputations of meaning to things that happen to us or around us. Because they affect our mood directly from moment to moment, they occupy a central role in CBT therapy.

Core Beliefs

These consist of the person's fundamental beliefs about himself, other people, or the world in general. These are not readily accessible to consciousness, couched in general statements, e.g., "People don't like me" or "The world is not a safe place," and are learned early in life from childhood experiences.

Dysfunctional Assumptions

Dysfunctional assumptions serve to bridge the gap between core beliefs and negative automatic thoughts. Considered guidelines for living, they are more specific in their use than core beliefs but more general than negative automatic thoughts. They follow an "If ... then ..." propositions and framed in "must" or "should" statements.

How Much of the TC Can be Considered Cognitive-Behavior Model?

To answer this, we have to examine some of the TC's philosophical beliefs, assumptions, and practices. TC's conceptualization of addiction, as a learned behavior that involves the whole person and manifested in the person's dysfunctional behavior, deficits in feelings (mood), and deficits in thinking (cognition), is consistent with behavior and cognitive-behavior theoretical views. The TC's contextual approach to understanding the problem and developing appropriate interventions to address the problem resonates with CBT's *interacting systems principle.* The TC environment provides the context where residents' behaviors are viewed and examined and then provided with feedback to help them develop self-awareness or insight to correct their problem. The person's difficulties are framed as comprising behavioral, emotional, and cognitive components within the social context of family, society, and other environmental influences.

The TC concept of the "here and now" is an existential-phenomenological perspective. However, it has a great deal of influence on the TC's view and treatment of addictive disorders which is consistent with CBT's perspective. TC considers current behavioral, emotional, and cognitive manifestations of the disorder as the immediate focus of intervention rather than delving on its etiology. Knowing the roots of the disorder does not change the fact that what happened in the past is causing you a problem, and the past might even provide a convenient excuse for failing to make a change. Historical information about the problem is brought in the context of what is happening now or how past events are continually being played out in the "here and now." When exploring past negative events in the lives of residents in TC groups or therapy, the details are less important than how those events shaped the person's beliefs, feelings, and coping strategies, bringing the focus of treatment on current behavior, feeling, and thinking.

Behavior therapy and CBT's influence on the TC is evident in the use of behavior-shaping tools, such as what used to be called the "verbal haircut," which is a direct verbal intervention by a group of peers for a member's poor behavior to elicit cognitive and attitudinal shift through *cognitive dissonance* (Festinger,1957). Dissonance is created by underscoring incongruence between the person's view of himself and his actual behavior. This process is mitigated by the underlying concern by his peers that such behavior might lead to more serious consequences if not curbed. Eliciting cognitive dissonance as a strategy to influence behavioral and attitudinal change is a staple of many of TC's community or group interventions, such as the Morning Meeting, General Meeting, or House Meeting, including the Intake Initial Interview and Peer Interventions.

To elicit behavioral change, the TC does not believe in the use of punishment, instead it employs the concept of "learning experience (LE)." This highly structured and educative intervention "facilitates connections between behaviors and their consequences," a set of skills in which many persons with addictive disorder and criminogenic propensities have serious deficits. A *Behavior Contract*, which is a more formalized form of the learning experience, is used for the same purpose of teaching "consequential thinking" and learning more adaptive coping skills. The overarching goal of LE is to teach consequential thinking. Above and beyond this is to provide the person opportunities to challenge self-imposed limitations or fears, such as feelings of inadequacy or fear of rejection by others. For example, a person might be given an LE for failing to wake up on time. His LE may involve rising an hour earlier and rousing the community on time. In addition, he will make observations of those who failed to get up on time and report them to his supervisors, a task he may feel anxious about for fear of getting ostracized by some of his peers.

TC's action oriented intervention is not only apparent in the use of "learning experiences." As mentioned above, regular practice of new skills or behavior is valued. It puts emphasis on behavior rehearsal or practicing new behavior, which at first may feel uncomfortable, but will eventually lead to behavioral, emotional, and cognitive integration, as exemplified in the famous TC slogan "act as if"- a strategy consistent with CBT's "behavioral principle." Some normative values which CBT deems important in therapeutic relationships, such as developing self-reliance, collaboration, self-competence and self-efficacy, are consistent with the TC's cornerstone principle of "community-as-method" and self-help philosophy.

Many TC concepts and interventions that have elements of behavior and cognitive-behavior therapy were developed independently from these models at first, but later elaborations on them contain traces of influences from both models.

New practices that some TCs have adopted as interventions, such as *Contingency Management* or *Motivational Incentives Therapy*, have deep roots in behavior theory. This evidence-based practice provides an excellent complement to the TC's "time-in-program-dependent" system of privileges as rewards. Whereas the privileges are earned based on length of time in the program and consistent performance of positive behavior, contingency management rewards target behaviors as they occur regardless of the person's program status (Perfas, 2012).

Interventions based on cognitive-behavior therapy, such as *relapse prevention, anger management, cognitive mapping, trauma counseling and group therapy*, and many others, have been blended into the TC treatment system. The marriage, however, has not been without its difficulties. The issue has not been with congruence between the two models, but of implementation that guarantees fidelity to practice for both models.

Another theory that resonates very well with the TC treatment philosophy and practices is social learning. The TC developed its treatment concepts and practices independent of social learning theory, although, it adapted many of its terminologies.

Bandura's Social Learning Theory

Albert Bandura's (1986) Social Learning Theory is based on the principles that people learn by watching what others do and that cognition or human thought processes play a central role in understanding personality. His theory provides a useful explanatory framework for understanding, predicting, and changing behaviors in the social environment of the TC. The social nature of learning is best exemplified in how TC residents learn behavioral, affective, and cognitive skills to improve personal competency in interpersonal relations, coping with challenging situations, and adopting the social norms and values of the TC.

Early in its development, the TC placed a large emphasis on the value of role-modeling behavior as a means of teaching more adaptive behaviors and influencing behavior change among residents. Role-model behavior means adopting the TC's social norms and exemplifying recovery-oriented behavior. Residents who demonstrate these expected behaviors are called "role-models," and those who occupy the upper echelon of the TC social hierarchy must be able to meet these expectations. Teaching new behaviors or concepts in TC is action oriented. Verbal commitments mean little compared to actualizing commitments in action.

Major Tenets of Social Learning Theory

The major tenets of Social Learning Theory can be summed up in the following:

- Learning occurs by observing others
- The same event may elicit different reactions from different individuals, or from the same individuals at different times
- The environment and an individual's behavior are interconnected
- Personal attributes are generated by the interactions of three factors: the environment, the behavior, and the person's psychic or cognitive processes

The last of these major concepts, provides an excellent framework for understanding how learning processes occur in the dynamic social environment of the TC. The three interactive and interdependent factors of *environment, behavior,* and *individual cognitive processes* constitute the entire learning context. They influence and control each other in a process called *reciprocal determinism* (Bandura, 1986), which explains how the environment and the person's personal attributes interact and determine his behavior and in turn impact others and his environment in a dynamic fashion. The dynamic process by which these factors interact creates the social learning context of the TC. This is illustrated in the following examples: a TC resident who is motivated to change helps himself and others by being a good example, which earns him a high social status in the TC social hierarchy. His role model behavior has helped create an environment of trust and responsible concern among his peers. On the other hand, a resident who shows poor treatment motivation and regularly disregards community rules has alienated his peers who are concerned about his destabilizing behavior and the unsafe environment his misbehavior has created. Figure 7.3 is a visual representation of reciprocal determinism.

Figure 7.3 Reciprocal Determinism

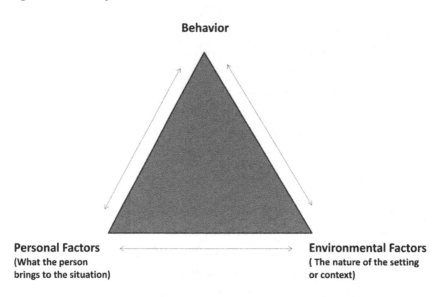

Behavior

Personal Factors
(What the person
brings to the situation)

Environmental Factors
(The nature of the setting
or context)

Four Major Components of the Modeling Process:

Attention

Attention plays a crucial role in learning something new. The more sa-lient the characteristics of the object of learning, the more likely they are to gain our attention. Moreover, if the object is deemed valuable or something that we can very well relate to, it is more likely to get our attention.

Retention

Not only is attending necessary in learning but one should be able to remember the object of attention. Rich images and the quality of the verbal description of the object contribute to retention.

Reproduction

The next step is the ability to translate what is learned into actual behavior.

Motivation

A rationale or a motive must drive one to imitate or copy the modeled behavior, which might be influenced by any or all of the following:

- Previous reinforcement
- Anticipated reinforcement
- Vicarious reinforcement

The Principles of Social Learning Theory as Applied in the TC

The following discussion illustrates in more details how the principles of Social Learning Theory operate in the TC and demonstrates the usefulness of the theory in explaining the learning process and how change occurs in its social context.

The observer is more likely to imitate the model's behavior if the model has qualities that the observer finds desirable.

In the TC, the role-models are extolled for behaviors that exemplify the recovery process. These behaviors are reinforced informally by the positive regard accorded to them by their peers and staff, and formally by promotions to a higher status in the social hierarchy. As such, they are effective role-models who are looked favorably upon by those aspiring to make progress in treatment and achieve similar social status.

Individuals are more likely to adopt a modeled behavior if the behavior has functional value and the model is someone they can identify with, relate to, and who possess coveted status.

The use of a person in recovery or formerly addicted individual as staff or role-model has been extensively utilized by TC to foster a sense of personal identification between the role-model and the newly recovering person. This provides a living example to emulate for those new to the recovery process. This not only facilitates better communication but also enhances the process of transmission of important recovery or treatment information from the upper social hierarchy down to the lower echelon of the TC.

Individuals will observe how role-models are treated based on their behavior. Model behaviors that are rewarded are likely to be imitated, while those that elicit punishment will be more likely to be avoided.

In the TC, new members often look up to the role-models or those in the upper echelon of the social hierarchy who earned their status through personal efforts and positive behavior. They imitate behaviors that were rewarded and earned them high status in the hierarchy, while avoiding behaviors that presented them with difficulties, such as getting demoted from their positions, subjected to behavioral sanctions, or given learning experiences.

Acquiring a behavior and performing the behavior are two different things. One can observe and learn the behavior but may not actualize it in action or may decide to execute it at some future time when the situation seems favorable.

Members or residents are constantly provided corrective feedback in the execution of their job functions, response to the treatment activities, or interactions with peers. Consequently, they are expected to demonstrate their learning or progress by rising in social status and by practicing role-model behavior. Not all do well or demonstrate behaviors that are consistent with the goals of recovery while in the TC. However, it is not unusual to get reports from some who dropped out or left treatment prematurely that they were able to practice some of the skills they learned during treatment to prevent relapse or pursue a more stable recovery process.

Coding modeled behavior into labels, words, or images facilitates better retention compared to mere observing.

The TC uses sets of "concepts," or philosophies, as tools to convey recovery principles coined as slogans such as: *"no free lunch;" "you alone can do it, but you can't do it alone;" "no pain, no gain;" "you can't keep it unless you give it away;" "what doesn't come out in the wash, comes out in the rinse;""responsible concern;" "pride in quality,"* etc.

These concepts embody the ideals, norms, and values of the TC which it believes are important in supporting the recovery process, and which residents should live by. These phrases are used liberally in seminars, in teaching new behavior, and in ordinary conversations to drive home a point or reinforce expected behaviors.

These slogans or "philosophies" are often posted in strategic places where residents congregate or meetings are held throughout the treatment facility.

Learning by observations involves four different processes which consist of attention, retention, motor production, and motivation reinforcement.
The TC employs different techniques to create salience by employing emotionally and thought-provoking rituals, language, and imagery, all designed to elicit attention, better retention, easy imitation, and motivation to follow through. The techniques are used in highly ritualized therapeutic activities, such as the morning meeting, house meeting, general meeting or community general assembly. These meetings are held to address behavioral issues in the community and to teach and reinforce community norms.

Teaching new skills to members follows a simple format consistent with social learning principles:
- Demonstrate the skill to be learned step by step
- Allow the person to do it himself
- Provide corrective feedback by reinforcing positive aspects of the behavior and correcting mistakes by additional demonstration
- Provide on-going supervision and reward

Attention and retention account for learning a target behavior, and motor production and motivation concern with the performance of the behavior.
In TC, to facilitate attention and retention of concepts and new behavior, the teacher must be credible and considered a role model in the community, and the target behavior must be relevant to the goal of recovery or helpful to the person in navigating the treatment process. This is accomplished by "elaborations" and ample examples. To encourage acting on or actualizing the desired behavior, actions such as taking initiative, taking positive risk, and having the right attitude towards the production of the target behavior, are rewarded.

Part II

An Overarching Theory for Grounding the Therapeutic Community: Attachment Theory

Attachment Theory is a perfect theory to ground the therapeutic community. Developed by John Bowlby (1969, 1973, 1980) and supported by studies conducted by Mary Ainsworth and her colleagues (Ainsworth, Blehar, Waters, & Wall, 1978), attachment theory is one of the most influential theories of development that has important implications for personality and psychopathology across the life span (Davila & Levy, 2006). The original theory provides a trans-theoretical perspective derived from Bowlby's interests in diverse disciplines of psychoanalysis, ethology, evolution, cognitive psychology, and developmental psychology. He borrowed principles from these disciplines to expound on "affectionate" bonding between infants and mothers or caregivers and how early attachment experiences have lasting effects on personality development, interpersonal style, emotional regulation, and the development of psychopathology. More recent studies incorporate neurophysiological perspectives to attachment theory. Moreover, attachment theory's focus on the psychobiological aspects of the attachment experience has lent legitimacy to many of Affect Regulation Theory's arguments (Flores, 2004).

Attachment Behavioral System

Attachment operates through the *Attachment Behavioral System*. A system comprised of different behaviors each of which may also serve other behavioral systems. The common feature that combines different behaviors into a behavioral system is that they serve a common outcome. In this case a predictable outcome, so that once the system is activated the predicted outcome is most likely to occur. The predictable outcome of the attachment behavioral system is to *deliver the individual into closer proximity or maintain proximity with his attachment figure* (mother or caregiver). Attachment-related behavior by infants, such as clinging, crying, smiling, monitoring caregivers, and developing preference for reliable caregivers or attachment figures, is a component of a functional biological system that improves the chances of protection from dangers (e.g., predators), obtaining comfort and support in times of adversity, and social learning.

A central notion to attachment theory is the nature of the bonding experience between the infant and the caregiver or attachment figure, who is normally the mother. The child will feel secure in his relationship with the attachment figure provided the attachment figure provides consistent, warm, and sensitive care. Conversely, when consistent, sensitive care is lacking, the child will feel insecure in his relationship with his attachment figure and will be unable to use the figure as a secure base to explore his environment and help him develop a stable sense of self (Prior & Glaser, 2006; Davila & Levy, 2006). These early attachment experiences or the lack thereof have profound consequences to the full development of the child and his patterns of adaptation throughout the life span.

More recent conceptualization of attachment theory argues that the survival gains of attachment is not only in effectively eliciting caregiver's protective response, but also in experiencing psychological regulation of negative affect states, which is necessary in the normal development of a coherent self (Fonagy, 1999). In a recent study, Wei and colleagues (2005), provide empirical support for attachment theory's assertion that different patterns of attachment are associated with different and distinct affect regulation strategies.

Patterns of Attachment

Ainsworth and colleagues (1978) documented different patterns of secure base use among children and their parents. These types or patterns were derived primarily from observations of the reactions of children to separation from, and subsequent reconciliation with, their caregivers. Ainsworth's (1969) simple and replicable *Strange Situation Test* (SST) evaluates the child's response to being separated from the primary caregiver and left alone or with a stranger for a three-minute period in a strange room. The patterns of responses that emerged correlated with observed maternal behavior toward children, which provide support for the role of parent-child relationship in the development of attachment patterns. There are four identified patterns of responses (Flores, 2004):

Securely attached children were more willing to seek reassurance from the caregiver after being reunited, and were easily comforted and willingly returned to exploratory play, whereas,

Insecure-Avoidant (or dismissing) children protested little at separation and tended to be more withdrawn or showed indifferent behavior toward the caregiver upon being reunited, and

Insecure-ambivalent (or preoccupied) children protested more at separation and were more distraught and harder to comfort, and vacillated between seeking proximity and expressing anger toward the caregiver, and finally,

Insecure-disorganized children showed no coherent pattern of response, either freezing or collapsing to the ground upon separation from caregiver. Upon reuniting with caregiver, they rock themselves vacantly in a corner.

Further data gathered from observations of children's responses to their caregiver in the Strange Situation Test, conducted in both the home and laboratory, established that the functions of attachment behaviors fall into three categories: *proximity maintenance* (physical closeness to caregiver), *safe haven* (a source of comfort in times of distress), and *secure base* (a reliable person who is there to lean on). If these important functions of attachment are not met, serious long-term consequences for the child's developing sense of self can occur (Flores, 2004).

Longitudinal studies on the influence of infant attachment styles on functioning and adaptation found that the attachment condition of one-year olds determined behavioral and representational processes in childhood, adolescence and later in life (Grossman & Grossman, 1991; Hamilton, 2000; Main & Cassidy, 1988; Sroufe, 1983; Waters, et al., 2000).

Main (1995), using a narrative interview, developed an assessment tool to determine adult attachment style. Using the *Adult Attachment Interview* (AAI), she found striking similarities between children and adult attachment styles. The findings indicated that patterns learned as children are retained throughout adulthood. To see the parallel findings between Ainsworth's *classification* and Main's narrative interview, the following table is presented (Flores, 2004):

Table 7.4 Ainsworth's and Main's Patterns of Attachment

SST (Ainsworth, et al., 1978)	AAI (Main, 1995) Attachment Narrative

Secure child   *Autonomous adult:*

"I feel safe to express my attachment needs, and I expect to have these needs met."

Insecure, resistant child   *Preoccupied adult:*

"Sometimes my needs are responded to, but more often than not they are not." "I must keep trying for more." "The responses never satisfy me."

Insecure, avoidant child   *Dismissive adult:*

"I will not let myself to feel I need others (although I do)." or "I convince myself that I'm getting what I want from others (even though I do not)."

Disorganized, disoriented child   *Unresolved adult:*

"My needs lead to loss or feeling afraid." "It is not safe to experience attachment feelings, (although I feel it), or think about it." "It is not safe to experience attachment feelings of loss (but I experience it anyway) because it arouses need and pain." "And if I feel attachment need and grief, this only leads to more loss and fear." "I'm caught in this vicious cycle."

Attachment Theory and Substance Abuse

Substantial literature exists that indicate the significant relationship between insecure attachment and substance abuse (Kassel, et al., 2007; Molnar, et al., 2010; Borhani, 2013). Brennan and Shaver (1995) reported that insecure attachment among college students was associated with frequency of alcohol use and drinking alcohol to relieve stress. Caspers and colleagues (2005) found a high prevalence of illicit substance use among those who were insecurely attached compared to individuals with secure attachment in their relationships. In another study of college students, Kassel and colleagues (2007) found insecure attachment to be significantly related to both frequency of substance use and stress-related use of substances, and the substance use appeared to be mediated largely by dysfunctional attitudes about the self and self-esteem. These findings lead to a possible etiological process linking insecure attachment and substance use, whereby insecurely attached individuals develop dysfunctional attitudes about themselves, which when these underlying insecurities are activated lead to depletion of self-esteem. Such feelings of low self-esteem lead to vulnerabilities for more substance abuse.

The significant relationships between attachment theory and affect regulation and a host of other psychopathologies have been studied extensively in the last two decades (Lay, K., et al., 1995; Mikulincer, M., et al., 2003; Wei, M., et al., 2005; Pietromonaco, P., et al., 2006). Difficulties in mood regulations and interpersonal problems associated with attachment-related anxiety or depression place certain individuals vulnerable to substance abuse as a coping strategy. Relevant findings from these studies provide valuable contributions in realigning the TC clinical program to become a science-based practice. The importance and relevance of this realignment is underscored by the increasing numbers of substance abuse clients in TC whose co-occurring disorders, such as trauma and PTSD, criminogenic personalities, personality disorders, among others, which are often impervious to traditional interventions, can be better understood and treated using attachment theory paradigm.

Flores (2004) considers addiction as a form of attachment disorder via the emotional regulation function of attachment. Individuals who have difficulty establishing emotionally regulating attachments are more likely to resort to drug and alcohol use as substitutes for their deficiency in intimacy. Dysfunctional attachment styles prevent individuals from having satisfactory experiences derived from interpersonal relationships and contribute to the formation of internal working models that perpetuate this condition. Substance abuse, therefore, can be viewed as a consequence of and solution for impaired attachment relationships. Further evidence for this is provided by Thorberg & Lyvers (2010) whose findings support broad attachment theory assumptions suggesting that attachment is associated with and predicts affect regulation abilities, difficulties with intimacy, and intrapersonal as well as interpersonal functioning in a sample of inpatient clients with substance use disorder. The findings make a strong case for the inclusion and assessment of attachment in the development of treatment programs for substance abusing individuals.

Attachment Theory and Treatment

Bowlby (1969, 1973, 1980) has conceptualized attachment theory to be relevant to both healthy and psychopathological development. He believed that insecure pattern of attachment, which originally is an adaptive set of strategies to manage distress, also predisposes the person to psychopathology and helps predict specific kinds of difficulties that can arise (Davila & Levy, 2006). Recent research supports his hypotheses and has linked attachment constructs to various symptoms and types of psychopathology, i.e., depression, anxiety, eating disorders, substance abuse and addiction, and other personality pathologies (Main, 1996; Jones, 1996; Davila, et al., 2005; Levy, 2005; Kassel, et al., 2007; Caspers, et al., 2006; Flores, 2004).

Bowlby argued that attachment theory has much to contribute to psychotherapy and has outlined the following main tasks for treatment (Davila and Levy, 2006):

Establishing a secure base. This requires providing clients with a secure base or a safe therapeutic environment from which they can explore the painful aspects of their life;

Exploring past attachments. This involves facilitating and helping clients explore past relationships and how they are intricately linked to current relationships, including their expectations, feelings, and behaviors;

Exploring the therapeutic relationship. This involves helping the client examine how the nature and quality of relationship with the therapist may be related to relationships or experiences outside of therapy;

Linking past experiences to present ones. This involves encouraging clients to develop new awareness of how current relationship experiences may be related to past ones; and

Revising internal working models. This involves helping clients take risks in new ways of feeling, thinking, and acting unlike in their past relationships.

The Internal Working Model

Bowlby's (1973) construct of *Internal Working Models* (IWM) is an important starting point in conceptualizing what the target of therapy or treatment might be. It is a representative model of internalization consistent with Piaget's theory (1954) of representation and also shares similarities to object relation's concepts of internalized self and object representations. Theoretically, it is closer to Intersubjectivity Theory (Stolorow et al., 1987) for its emphasis on how interpersonal field is created by individuals involved within a relationship. The emotional accessibility of the caregiver is the defining factor that determines the makeup of an internal working model. How the caregiver is perceived by the child is more important than what the caregiver does – the experience of being with the child defines the nature of the relationship-- which is what is internalized and not just the object or self-representation. According to

Bowlby's IWM construct, the primary unit of existence is not the self and object representation, "but the relationship and the rules that govern that relationship," which is stored in the "implicit memory" not accessible via normal cognition. Through repeated experiences, the child develops sets of expectations from the caregiver. It is the rules governing these expectations that are internalized together with mental representations that guide the person's thoughts, feelings, and behavior in subsequent relationships –"how I have to be in order to stay in a relationship with you"- defines the structure of the IWM and dictates the patterns of subsequent attachment-relevant relationships (Flores, 2004).

Maladaptive working models can be determined from repetitive, dysfunctional thinking, and emotional and behavioral patterns, which can be the target of therapeutic interventions. Davila and Levy (2006) pointed out that the therapeutic tasks that Bowlby (1988) have identified are consistent with the major treatment components designed to achieve change by various treatment approaches. These are outlined below:

- Fostering positive expectancies for change, i.e., helping client develop motivation for change, etc.
- Fostering effective therapeutic alliance between client and therapist, e.g., empathic relationship between client and therapist, agreement on treatment goals and interventions, etc.
- Enhancing awareness, about thoughts, feelings, and behavior.
- Facilitating corrective experience, e.g., helping clients take risks in practicing new behaviors and experiencing them differently.
- Helping clients to be continually grounded in reality and generalizing the outcome to other life areas.

****

The preceding discussion is a basic outline of attachment theory that focused on its potential applications to the clinical goals of the therapeutic community. It holds promise for the TC's future treatment direction, but more importantly, it reinforces many of the TC's treatment principles and practices, especially the emphasis on establishing a safe and caring social environment; using "a caring community" as a safe base for exploring new ways of behaving, feeling, and thinking; developing relationships based on genuine caring and self-understanding; and in traditional TC groups, the focusing on the impact of past experiences and relationships on self-concept and substance abuse. Unfortunately, many of these traditional groups have been largely abandoned in the practice of most TCs in the U.S.

Some of the TC's old and crude conceptualizations (e.g., reshaping the fractured self of the addict by breaking him down and rebuilding the person back with "care and concern" and based on new self-understanding, casting away false self-images, etc.) were not totally without merit. All of these resonate very well with the attachment theory's belief of grounding a pathological internal working model on reality. A similar concept is the *encapsulation* of addicted individuals, which we now know arises from very early insecure attachment experience with the caregiver. Attachment theory provides the appropriate language and voice to articulate experientially-based native TC theories, which are more intuitive than cognitive in character. The TC's use of rituals and techniques that evoked and appealed on "implicit memory," more than a reliance on the cognitive conscious processes, to release conflicted emotions that have roots in the past and shed light on present difficulties, were ahead of its time. Take for example the use of music tied to a certain era and the use of heavy symbolism during a marathon group, they were both powerful tools that penetrated otherwise impregnable realms to expand the group members' awareness.

The TC's traditional emphasis of creating a sense of family among residents and establishing healthy relationships based on a new self-understanding and grounded in reality have provided a protective buffer from the risk of drug relapse. Relationships forged during treatment in TC are often lasting and provide the needed positive support system, especially for those with limited sources of social support. These relationships grow out of strong bonds that developed while sharing common struggles, learning how to develop healthier attachments, and re-learning the ability to manage difficult emotions with the support of others.

Chapter 8

A Revitalized Treatment Agenda for the Therapeutic Community

The following is a bold proposal for revitalizing the treatment direction that the TC should take based on what we know about addiction from an attachment theory paradigm, and what have been proven to work based on evidence-based practices. For starters, let us review some treatment principles for addiction from attachment theory perspective.

Principles for Treating Addiction as an Attachment Disorder

Flores (2004) provides principles that can serve as an addiction treatment guide from an attachment theory paradigm:

- Humans need each other for purposes of regulating each other's emotions.
- Attachment is not reducible to a secondary drive; like social mammals, humans are biologically hard-wired to need people. Evolution favored mechanisms that promoted parent-offspring proximity in an environment of evolutionary adaptation.

- Secure attachment is liberating. The stronger the earliest attachment experience, the greater the freedom from excessive need for external sources of affect regulation; consequently, as adults, relationships will be more rewarding which decrease the propensity to turn to substances as means of emotional regulation.

- Those who develop insecure or dysfunctional attachment due to inadequate early attachment experiences are more vulnerable and more likely to resort to other sources of external regulation, such as substance use or other objects of obsessive-compulsive behavior.

- Chronic, prolonged substance abuse, which is a misguided attempt at self-repair, can produce alterations in an already vulnerable person's brain, exacerbating existing attachment and interpersonal difficulties, and further compromising any interpersonal skills the person may have prior to regular substance abuse.

- Unless healthy forms of affect regulation are developed, addicted individuals will always be vulnerable to one form of addiction or another. So long as the addicted person remains attached to substances, he will never find other forms of affect regulation.

- An important requirement of early stage recovery is total abstinence from the object of addiction (be it a thing, an activity, or person).

- Long-term treatment must be geared in altering the substance abusers' internal working model that would effectively transform the "implicit" rules that guide all of their intimate relationships.

Understanding How and Why the TC Works from an Attachment Theory Perspective

From an attachment theory perspective, the TC works because of the fundamental principle that "exposure to people changes people." More specifically, powerful attachment experiences have the ability to alter a person's nervous system. We know from research that intense and salient emotionally charged experiences, whether substance or naturally induced, have the potential to alter how the brain is wired. In treatment, individuals in attachment relationships, with some help, learn to regulate their nervous system and unconsciously acquire implicit knowledge of the rules involve in healthy relationships. Attachment provides stabilizing influences on individuals. Extended exposure to powerful attachment environments, such as what the TC provides, can shape patterns of relationship that become ingrained in implicit memory, altering individuals' internal working models and re-configuring old rules that guide their behaviors in relationships (Flores, 2004). Amini (1996) believes that healthy attachment environment not only alters old patterns of relatedness, it also provides lasting memory for new and healthier representations.

The following are some of the reasons why and how the TC works:

- The therapeutic community works because it harnesses our fundamental nature as social beings. "Wounded," humans tend to seek other human beings for healing - addiction hurts, not just physically; the entire person suffers psychologically, socially, and spiritually. There is a social context to addiction, which involves the people around the addicted individual who feel cheated and betrayed. Socially-based emotions of shame and guilt haunt the addicted individual and create added burden to the already battered self-esteem. If healing from addiction is to occur, it needs to be within a social context in which the TC can provide the addicted person a favorable environment to work through his problem with his own self and his relationships with others.

- The social context is the "community" where the addicted individual can find solace in the knowledge that he is not alone. This group helps moderate his intense negative feelings related to his failed effort to repair himself by indulging in substance abuse. The social learning environment of the TC, with its structure and social hierarchy, affords the member opportunities to learn about himself through his intimate interactions with peers and staff, whether in groups, social activities, or in his work assignments.

- The sense of community that the group provides is a safe haven where the person can develop multiple attachment figures based on mutual concern. This allows him to explore and work through the intense feelings of anger, hostility, ambivalence, etc. related to his failed relationships, with less fear of being swallowed by these overpowering emotions. Instead, he is provided with appropriate feedback and dependable emotional support.

- The community ensures that members remain abstinent from substance use, while providing them with opportunities to experience anxiety and frustrations in a more natural, albeit controlled environment. These experiences will provoke them to exhibit their typical self-destructive and maladaptive behavioral patterns and coping style, while the community provides support and assurance that they do not act out and lose control, until they learn to cope with stressful situations in a more productive fashion.

- The various group processes and community meetings are forums where members can explore difficult emotions related to past relationships in multiple types and levels of transferences, in the safety of the community.

- "Community spirit" is the cohesive force that binds members to the TC. It facilitates integration and affiliation to the community, holding in abeyance the urge to leave treatment prematurely. Sense of community or "community spirit" is to the TC what cohesiveness is to group psychotherapy (Ormont, 1992). Both provide the necessary mechanism and conditions for harnessing group dynamics to promote change. As Flores (2004) states, within this context, myriads of relationships are possible – member-to-member, member-to-group, and member-to-staff – which provide opportunities for individual members to reveal deficits in attachment styles, while providing a therapeutic culture that can be reparative.

- The TC with its shared pro-social norms and values, culture of recovery, and healthy lifestyle, offers an alternative to what the addicted-person has been used to during his years of addiction. This reparative condition is necessary for the person to reinvent himself and develop a new basis of relatedness with others.

Burlingame and colleagues (2001), in a review of literature examining results of "member-to-member" and "member-to-group" group interactions, have established the following relationships between cohesion and successful treatment as empirically validated. These outcomes resonate with observations made about the TC processes and provide avenues for possibly generalizing them to the therapeutic community:

- Clients who reported high levels of connections or attachments, such as feeling understood, safe, and comfortable in the group, also reported the most improvements in their symptoms.

- Clients' self-report of liking the group, experiencing intimacy, feeling accepted, and experiencing warmth, empathy, friendliness, consideration, genuineness, and working together to solve problems were found to be related to improvements.

- Treatment retention in group by members, particularly at the early stage of group treatment, is related to feeling attracted to the group, even a little.

- High dropout rates were related to poor outcome.

- From an individual observer's ratings, the significant relationship between "level of group cohesion" (e.g., non-involvement vs. involvement, trust vs. mistrust) and "self-reported improvement and cohesion" exhibited during the first thirty minutes of a session, produced the best outcome results.

- Those members who felt personally validated and understood by a group leader showed greater improvements. Whereas, those who reported negative feelings and experiences with a group leader were associated with poorer outcomes.

- The higher the member's positive attachment to the group and its members, the greater the member's disclosure which resulted to more intense feedback from members, which in turn facilitated more interactions and more positive outcome.

- The earlier group cohesion begins to emerge, the better the group's capacity to manage and tolerate conflict.

A Revitalized TC Program

The tasks for psychotherapy that Bowlby has outlined fit very nicely with the treatment goals of the TC. Although he conceptualized them in terms of traditional psychotherapy, it is not difficult to extrapolate and make them relevant to residential treatment, such as the therapeutic community. Attachment theory and its basic principles provide the foundation for establishing the TC's therapeutic environment and the practice of many of its traditional group processes, e.g., *initial or emotional interview, static group, psychosocial probe, extended group*, and *marathon group*, as well as in individual work with clients (See Perfas, 2012 for descriptions of these TC interventions).

The goals of the traditional TC group processes are compatible with and should be grounded in the principles of attachment theory. This theory also complements social learning and cognitive-behavior theories which inform the practice of the TC behavior-shaping interventions.

Two of the distinct and overlapping categories of TC interventions are the *behavior-shaping tools* and the *emotional/psychological interventions* (See Chapter 3). The traditional TC behavior-shaping tools are largely grounded in social learning and cognitive-behavior theories. With minor adjustments, the practice or applications of these tools can be easily made to conform, if they have not already, to the aforementioned theories. The major emphasis of these tools is on behavioral accountability which should be mitigated by humane practice of responsible care and concern.

The emotional/psychological tools that include the traditional TC group processes, which have been mostly abandoned in many American TCs, can be resurrected, modified, and modernized so that their practice is consistent with the knowledge and understanding provided by attachment theory. In principle, the goals of *static groups, probes, extended groups*, and *marathons* have always been the reconciliation of the addicted person's many unresolved lifelong problems with himself and others. The focus is on achieving insight and awareness and accessing and re-experiencing "forgotten" memories and feelings in a different light. The underlying assumptions are based on what was believed to be the addict's dysfunctional view of himself (and the world) that stemmed from the past. These assumptions can now be refined using sound theory. Moreover, the increasing demand in drug treatment to concurrently treat common co-occurring psychiatric disorders, particularly trauma, can now be addressed more fully under this new agenda.

While the cognitive-behavioral approaches inform TC practices that are directed to behavioral and cognitive change, such as the behavior-shaping tools and some CBT-oriented groups, a revitalized TC groups can address the more deeply rooted "unconscious" psycho-biological issues related to problematic patterns of attachment, deficits related to emotional regulation, and faulty internal working models. Attachment theory offers more in depth elaborations of CBT's hallmark cognitive concepts of "levels of cognition" (i.e., automatic negative thoughts, core beliefs, and dysfunctional assumptions) by offering compelling etiological explanations for these cognitive patterns.

References

Aisnworth, M.S., Blehar, M.C., Waters, E., & Wall, S. (1978). *Patterns of attachment: A psychological study of the Strange Situation*. Hillsdale, NJ: Erlbaum.

Amini, F. (1996). *Attachment Theory and Group Psychotherapy*. American Group Psychotherapy Association, 35th Annual Conference. February 23. San Francisco, CA.

ATCA Publication, (2013). Towards better practice in therapeutic communities. Appendix 1, ATCA. www.atca.com.au.

Bandura, L. (1986). *Social foundation of thought and action*. Englewood Cliffs, N.J.: Printice-Hall.

Baumeister, R.F. & Leary, M.R. (1995). The need to belong: Desire for interpersonal attachments as a fundamental human motivation. *Psychological Bulletin,* 117, 497-529.

Belding, M.A., Iguchi, M.Y., Morral, A.R., et al. (1997). Assessing the helping alliance and its impact in the treatment of opiate dependence. *Drug and Alcohol Dependence,* 48:51-59.

Bloom, S. (1997). *Creating sanctuary: Toward the evolution of sane societies*. New York: Routledge.

Borhani, Y. (2013). Substance abuse and insecure attachment styles: A relational study, *LUX: A Journal of Transdisciplinary Writing and Research* from Claremont Graduate University: Vol. 2: Iss. 1, Article 4.

Bowlby, J. (1969). *Attachment and loss:* Vol. 1. *Attachment.* New York: Basic Books

Bowlby, J. (1973). *Attachment and loss*: Vol. 2. *Separation: Anxiety and anger.* New York: Basic Books.

Bowlby, J. (1980). *Attachment and loss*: Vol. 3. *Loss.* New York: Basic Books.

Brehm, J. (1966). *A theory of psychological reactance.* New York: Academic Press.

Brill, L., Lieberman, L., & Green, S.S. (1969). *Authority and addiction.* Boston: Little Brown & Company.

Burlingame, G.M, Fuhriman, A., & Johnson, J.E. (2001). Cohesion in group psychotherapy. *Psychotherapy*, 38, 373-384.

Caspers, K.M., Yucuis, R., Troutman, B., & Spinks, R. (2006). Attachment as an organizer of behavior: Implications for substance abuse problem and willingness to seek treatment. *Substance Abuse Treatment, Prevention, and Policy*, 1: 1-32.

Clark, H.W., Masson, C.L., Delucchi, K.L., et al. (2001). Violent traumatic events and drug abuse severity. *Journal of Substance Abuse Treatment*, 20:121-127.

Davila, J., Ramsay, M., Stroud, K.B., & Steinberg, S.J. (2005). Attachment. In B. Hankin & J. Abela (Eds.), *Development of psychopathology: A vulnerability-stress perspective* (pp. 215-242). Thousand Oaks, CA: Sage.

Davila, J. & Levy, K. (2006). Introduction to the special section of attachment theory and psychotherapy. *Journal of Consulting and Clinical Psychology*. Vol. 74, 6, 989-993.

Deitch, D. (1992). *The therapeutic community trainer's guide*. New York: Daytop International.

De Leon, G. (2000). *The therapeutic community: Theory, model, and method*. New York: Springer Publishing Company.

De Leon, G. & Melnick, G. (1993). *Therapeutic Community Scale of Essential Elements Questionnaire (SEEQ)*. New York City: Community Studies Institute, 2nd World Trade Center, 16th Floor 10048.

Dom, G., De Wilde, B., Hulstijn, W., Sabbe, B. (2007). Traumatic experiences and posttraumatic stress disorders: differences between treatment-seeking early- and late-onset alcoholic patients. *Compr Psychiatry*, 48:178-185.

Festinger, L. (1957). *A theory of cognitive dissonance*. Illinois: Row and Peterson.

Flores, P.J. (2004). *Addiction as an attachment disorder*. New York: Jason Aronson.

Fonagy, P. (1999). Attachment, the development of the self, and its pathology in personality disorder. In J. Derksen & C. Maffei Dordrecht (Eds.), *Treatment of personality disorders* (pp.53-68). Dordrecht, the Netherlands: Kluwer Academic.

Glaser, F. B. (1978). The origin of the drug-free therapeutic community: A retrospective history. *Addict Ther.* (Special issues 3 & 4): 3-15.

Grossman, K.E. & Grossman, K. (1991). Attachment quality as an organizer of emotional and behavioral responses in a longitudinal perspective. In C. M. Parkes, J. Stevenson-Hinde, & P. Marris (Eds.). *Attachment across the life cycle* (pp. 93-114). New York: Tavistock/ Routledge.

Hamilton, C.E. (2000). Continuity and discontinuity of attachment from infancy through adolescence. *Child Development, 71,* 690-694.

Higgins, S.T. & Petry, N.M. (1999). Contingency management: Incentive for sobriety. *Alcohol Research & Health,* 23(2): 122-127.

Janzen, R. (2001). *The rise and fall of Synanon: A California utopia.* Baltimore: Johns Hopkins University Press.

Joe, G.W., Simpson, D.D., Dansereau, D.F., & Rowan-Szal, G.A. (2001). Relationship between counseling rapport and drug abuse treatment outcomes. *Psychiatric Services,* 52(9): 1223-1229.

Jones, E.E. (1996). Introduction to the special section on attachment and psychopathology: Part I. *Journal of Consulting and Clinical Psychology, 64,* 5-7.

Kassel, J.D., Wardle, M., & Roberts, J.E. (2007). Adult attachment security and college student substance use. *Addictive Behaviors, 32,* 1164-1176.

Kooyman, M. (1992). *The therapeutic community for addicts: Intimacy, parent involvement, and treatment outcome.* Rotterdam: Erasmus University.

Kooyman, M. (1993). *The therapeutic community for addicts: Intimacy, parent involvement and treatment outcome.* Lisse, the Netherlands: Swets & Zeitlinger.

Kooyman, M. (2001). The history of therapeutic communities: A view from Europe. In B. Rawlings and R. Yates, (Eds). *Therapeutic communities for the treatment of drug users.* London: Jessica Kingsley Publishers.

Lay, K., Waters, E., Posada, G., & Ridgeway, D. (1995). Attachment security, affect regulation, and defensive response to mood induction. In E. Waters, B. Vaughn, G. Posada, and K. Kondo-Ikemura (Eds.). *Caregiving, Cultural, and Cognitive Perspectives on Secure-Base Behavior and Working Models: New Growing Points of Attachment Theory and Research.* Monographs of the Society for Research in Child Development, 60 (2-3, Serial no. 244), 179-196.

Levy, K. N. (2005). The implications of attachment theory and research for understanding borderline personality disorder. *Development and Psychopathology,17,* 959-986.

Lloyd, C.F. and O'Callaghan, F.V. (2001). The therapeutic communities for the treatment of addictions in Australia. In B. Rawlings and R. Yates, (Eds). *Therapeutic communities for the treatment of drug users.* London: Jessica Kingsley Publishers.

Main, M. (1996). Introduction to the special section on attachment and psychopathology: 2. Overview of the field of attachment. *Journal of Consulting and Clinical Psychology, 64,* 237-243.

Main, M. & Cassidy, J. (1988). Categories of response to reunion with the parent at age 6: Predictable from infant attachment classifications and stable over a 1-month period. *Developmental Psychology, 24,* 415-426.

Maslow, A. H. (1954). *Motivation and personality.* New York: Harper and Row.

Maslow, A. H. (1976). *The farther reaches of human nature.* New York: Penguin Books.

Matua Raki Report (2012). *Supporting New Zealand's therapeutic community workforce: An investigation of current needs.* Ministry of Health, New Zealand.

Mikulincer, M., Shaver, P.R., Pereg, D. (200). Attachment theory and affect regulation: The dynamics, development, and cognitive consequences of attachment-related strategies. *Motivation and Emotion,* 27(2):77-102.

Mills, K.L., Lynskey, M., Teesson, M., *et al.* (2005). Posttraumatic stress disorder among people with heroin dependence in the Australian treatment outcome study (ATOS): prevalence and correlates. *Drug Alcohol Dependence,* 77:243-249.

Molnar, D. S., Sadava, S.W., De Courville, N.H., Perrier, C. (2010). Attachment, motivations, and alcohol: Testing a dual-path model of high-risk drinking and adverse consequences in transitional clinical and student samples. *Canadian Journal of Behavioural Science/Revue canadienne des sciences du comportement,* 42 (1): 1-13.

Najavits, L. (2002). *Seeking safety: A treatment manual for PTSD and substance abuse.* New York: The Guilford Press.

Norlin, M.N. & Chess, W.A. (1997). *Human behavior and the social environment.* Boston: Allyn and Baccon.

O'Brien, W.B. & Perfas, F.B. (2002). The therapeutic community. In: J. Lowenson; P. Ruiz; R. Millman & J. Langrod. (Eds.) *Substance abuse: A comprehensive textbook.* Fourth Edition. New York: Lippincott Williams & Wilkens.

Ormont, L. (1992). *The group therapy experience.* New York: St. Martin Press.

Pearce, S. & Pickard, H. (2012). How therapeutic communities work: Specific factors related to positive outcome. *International Journal of Social Psychiatry*, o(o) 1-10.

Perfas, F. (2002). *Drug abuse: Causal attributions by policy stakeholders.* Ann Arbor, MI: (UMI) ProQuest Information and Learning (Doctoral thesis).

Perfas, F. (2004). *Therapeutic community: A social system perspective.* New York: iUniverse Inc.

Perfas, F. (2012). *Deconstructing the therapeutic community: A handbook for addiction professionals.* New York: Hexagram Publishing.

Perfas, F. & Spross, Z. (2007). Why the concept-based therapeutic community can no longer be called drug free. *Journal of Psychoactive Drugs*, March 2007.

Petry, N.M. (2000). A comprehensive guide to the application of contingency management procedures in clinical settings. *Drug and Alcohol Dependence*, 58, 9-25.

Piaget, J. (1954). *The construction of reality in the child.* New York: Basic Books.

Pietromonaco, P., Feldman-Barrett, L., Powers, S.I. (2006). Adult attachment theory and affective reactivity and regulation. In D.K. Snyder, J.A. Simpson, & J.N. Hughes (Eds.). *Emotion regulation in couples and families: Pathways to dysfunction and health.* Washington D.C.: American Psychological Association.

Prior, V. & Glaser, D. (2013). *Understanding attachment and attachment disorders: Theory, evidence, and practice.* London: Jessica Kingsley Publishers.

Rapoport, R.N. (1960). *Community as doctor.* London: Tavistock Publications.

Reynolds, M., Mezey, G., Chapman, M., et al. (2005). Co-morbid post-traumatic stress disorder in a substance misusing clinical population. *Drug Alcohol Dependence, 77*:251-258.

Rowan-Szal, G.A., Greener, J.M., Roark, R., & Simpson, D.D. (2000, April). *Demonstration of a contingency management system (TCU Cookie Chart).* Presented at the AMTA Methadone Conference, San Francisco, CA.

SAMHSA (2010). Results from 2009 National Survey on Drug Use and Health: Mental health findings. *Office of Applied Studies, NSDUH Series H-39,* NO. SMA 10-4609.

Simpson, D.D. (2004). A conceptual framework for drug treatment process and outcomes. *Journal of Substance Abuse Treatment, 27,* 99-121.

Soyez, V. & Broekaert, E. (2005). Therapeutic communities, family therapy, humanistic psychology: History and current examples. *Journal of Humanistic Psychology, 45*:302-333.

Sroufe, L.A. (1983). Infant-caregiver attachment and patterns of adaptation in pre-school: The roots of maladaptation and competence. In M. Perlmutter (Ed.). *The Minnesota Symposia on Child Psychology: Vol. 16. Development and policy concerning children with special needs* (pp. 41-83). Hillsdale, NJ: Erlbaum.

Stolorow, R, Brandchaft, B., & Atwood, G. (1987). *Psychoanalytic treatment: An intersubjective approach*. Hillsdale, NJ: Analytic Press.

Stringer, C. (2012).). *Lone survivors: How we came to be the only humans on earth*. New York: Times Books.

Sugarman, B. (1974). *Daytop Village: A therapeutic community*. New York: Holt, Rinehart and Winston, Inc.

Tangney, J.P. & Dearing, R.L. (2002). *Shame and guilt*. New York: The Guilford Press.

Thorberg, F. & Lyvers, M. (2010). Attachment in relation to affect regulation and interpersonal functioning among substance use disorder inpatients. *Addiction research and theory, 18*(4), 464-478

Vanderplasschen, W., Colpaert, K., Antrique, M., Rapp, R. C., Pearce, S., Broekaert, E., and Vandevelde, S. (2013). Therapeutic communities for addictions: A review of their effectiveness from a recovery-oriented perspective. *The Scientific World Journal*, Vol. 2013.

Vandevelde, S. (1999). *Maxwell Jones and his works in the therapeutic community*. (thesis). Ghent University, Belgium. *archive.pettrust.org.uk*.

Warren-Holland, D. (2006). *The development of "concept" houses in Great Britain and Ireland, 1967-1976*.

Waters, E., Merrick, S., Treboux, D., Crowell, J., & Albersheim, L. (2000). Attachment security in infancy and early childhood: A 20-year longitudinal study. *Child Development, 71*, 684-689.

Wei, M., Vogel, D.L., Ku, T., Zakalik, R.A. (2005). Adult attachment, affect regulation, negative mood, and interpersonal problems: The mediating roles of emotional reactivity and emotional cutoff. *Journal of Counseling Psychology,* 52(2): 14-24.

Westbrook, D., Kennerley, H., & Kirk, J. (2011). *An introduction to cognitive behavior therapy* (2nd edition). London: Sage Publications.

White, W. (1993). *Critical incidents: Ethical issues in substance abuse prevention and treatment.* Illinois: Lighthouse Training Institute.

Woodhams, A. (2001). The staff member in the therapeutic community. In B. Rawlings and R. Yates. (Eds.), *Therapeutic communities for the treatment of drug users.* London: Jessica Kingsley Publishers.

Yablonsky, L. (1965). *Synanon: The tunnel back.* New York: Macmillan.

Yablonsky, L. (1989). *The therapeutic community: A successful approach for treating substance abusers.* New York: Gardner Press, Inc.

Yalom, I.D. (1995). *The Theory and Practice of Group Psychotherapy.* 4th Edition. New York: Basic Books.

Appendix

Survey of Practice Principles of the Therapeutic Community

USING THE RATING SCALE BELOW, PLEASE RATE HOW MUCH OF THE PRACTICE PRINCIPLES ARE APPLIED IN YOUR TC PROGRAM:

A. TREATMENT STRUCTURE	NOT AT ALL			A LOT	
1. Use of Treatment Phases and Treatment Plan	1	2	3	4	5
2. A ritual for joining the community (Initial Interview)	1	2	3	4	5
3. An orientation & engagement process to the program for new members	1	2	3	4	5
4. A ritual for separating from the community (Discharge Plan)	1	2	3	4	5
5. Use of Social Hierarchy and Structure of Responsibility	1	2	3	4	5

B. TREATMENT CONDITION	NOT AT ALL			A LOT	
1. An emotionally and physically safe environment	1	2	3	4	5
2. Dynamic and Pervasive Treatment Process (24/7 structure)	1	2	3	4	5
3. Peer Driven (Peer holding peer accountable)	1	2	3	4	5

		NOT AT ALL				A LOT
4.	Culture of self-help and mutual help	1	2	3	4	5
5.	Shared community norms and values	1	2	3	4	5

C. STAFF'S ROLE AND FUNCTION

		NOT AT ALL				A LOT
1.	Trans-disciplinary staff process	1	2	3	4	5
2.	Staff as Role Model and Rational Authority	1	2	3	4	5
3.	Application of "community as method" through the three levels of staff operation	1	2	3	4	5
4.	System for training and supervising the social hierarchy and levels of responsibility	1	2	3	4	5

D. BIOPSYCHOSOCIAL TREATMENT INTERVENTIONS

		NOT AT ALL				A LOT
1.	Graduated system of application of behavior-shaping tools & sanctions to correct deviant behaviors	1	2	3	4	5
2.	Structured reward system of privileges & motivational incentives	1	2	3	4	5
3.	Medical and mental health services to assess, intervene, and monitor medical and psychiatric conditions that co-occur with substance abuse	1	2	3	4	5
4.	Psychological interventions that promote emotional growth	1	2	3	4	5
5.	Activities that enhance intellectual abilities, self-awareness, moral reasoning, and self-actualization	1	2	3	4	5
6.	Activities that increase personal competency & survival skills	1	2	3	4	5

		NOT AT ALL				A LOT
7.	Activities that promote pro-social values & social reintegration	1	2	3	4	5
8.	A family program that engages & provides support for families & significant others	1	2	3	4	5

E. TREATMENT OUTCOME AND FEEDBACK

		NOT AT ALL				A LOT
1.	There is a system for monitoring & evaluating program effectiveness and outcome	1	2	3	4	5

Index

About the Author

Dr. Fernando B. Perfas has over forty years experience in the field of addiction, most of which has been spent in therapeutic community (TC) work. This is his fourth book about the TC. In the last twenty years he has been a trainer and consultant of the TC here in the U.S. as well as overseas. He has conducted training in more than thirty-five countries for both government and non-government drug treatment agencies, including community-based and prison-based therapeutic communities. He earned his bachelor's and master's degrees at the *Pamantasan Ng Lungsod Ng Maynila* (University of the City of Manila), a counseling degree at University of Missouri, Kansas City, and a doctorate in social welfare at Adelphi University in New York. He worked for Daytop Village for many years and a few years for Phoenix House in New York. The author can be reached at perfas@earthlink.net or fbperfas@gmail.com